"Bioethics and Medicine: A Short Companion, written in the Christian Hippocratic tradition of Ramsey, Pellegrino, and Meilaender, is one of those little books that help profoundly crystalize one's thinking about this complex moral field. Mitchell's mature reflections serve as a most useful prolegomena to modern bioethics' underlying timeless principles. Hot-button topics are clearly and faithfully explicated. Mitchell's recounting of evangelicals' often uncritical acceptance of contraception and assisted reproductive technologies helps inform our contemporary debates. I wish I could have read this book before starting medical school forty-four years ago."

—**Don W. Buckley**, MD, research fellow, Ethics and Religious Liberty Commission

"Ben Mitchell is to be congratulated on a tour de force, corralling the top ethical challenges confronting us all in medicine and medical science, and the top thinkers—beginning, of course, with the greatest of them all, who continues to haunt medical practice even today: Hippocrates of Cos. Pastors, students, physicians, and all the rest of us now have the best possible guide to human life, health, and ethics for today and tomorrow."

—**Nigel M. de S. Cameron**, president emeritus, Center for Policy on Emerging Technologies, Washington, DC

"A journey into the heart of Christian tradition regarding the work of medicine. Mitchell offers a Christian Hippocratism for our times."

—**Farr Curlin**, MD, Josiah C Trent Professor of Medical Humanities; professor of Medicine; co-director of Theology, Medicine, and Culture Initiative, Duke University

"Based on a lifetime of reflection and teaching, Dr. Mitchell's excellent book addresses a broad range of bioethical and medical concerns to help guide Christians to make sense of some of the most fundamentally important aspects of our lives as embodied souls. This carefully crafted work is penetrating and accessible, and it's seasoned with personal narratives, full of historical insights, and responsive to current debates. It engages the practical ethical challenges we face as patients while also illuminating the responsibilities of health-care professionals wanting to follow God's pattern of covenantal love by caring for patients as persons. I recommend this book highly, for patients and professionals alike."

—**Lauris Kaldjian**, MD, director, Program in Bioethics and Humanities; Richard M. Caplan Chair in Biomedical Ethics and Medical Humanities; professor, internal medicine, University of Iowa

"Physician morale is at an all-time low, with burnout at an all-time high. The Association of American Medical Colleges predicts a shortage of over 100,000 physicians in the next ten years. Why is this? As Mitchell writes, medicine has lost its way. Fortunately, *Bioethics and Medicine* points the way back to a rightly ordered way for medicine to reclaim its rich roots in the Hippocratic tradition and for both the patient and the physician to flourish."

—**Jennifer Lahl**, BSN, RN, founder, Center for Bioethics and Culture

"Like all of Ben Mitchell's work, this book is a gift to the church. It is simple and accessible in concept but deep and insightful in content. Ben's commitment to biblical fidelity and life-honoring moral reasoning makes this a trustworthy book for those just entering the discussion as well as those wanting deeper insights into some of the more important foundations and principles of medical ethics."

—**Mark Liederbach**, senior professor of ethics, theology, and culture, Southeastern Baptist Theological Seminary

"At a time when the practice of medicine has often succumbed to the spirit of our age, emphasizing a radical autonomy and a consumer mindset at the expense of genuine caregiving, a Christian understanding of human beings as a foundation for the practice of health care is desperately needed. This introduction is a must read for thoughtful Christians, especially pastors and Christians in medical fields. Drawing from personal clinical experience and careful research and reflection, Mitchell brings a unique and thoughtful perspective to bioethics while combining philosophical, theological, and biblical reflection with compassionate pastoral and clinical care. In this concise treatment, he lays a crucial foundation and offers helpful application to some of the critical issues of our day at the edges of life. This is a must read!"

—**Ken Magnuson**, executive director,
Evangelical Theological Society

"The bedside of illness is a holy space. But prayerful and conscientious physicians today—whether early in training or seasoned in practice—have little time to reflect on the potentially lethal impact of prevailing secular bioethics on the care of their patients, from conception to life's prime to the hour of death. Drawing from Scripture, orthodox theology, and the work of key Christian bioethicists of our time, Dr. Mitchell orients his readers to the clinical ethical issues of our daily work and offers an approach to these that compassionately honors the patient, who is a 'sacredness.' This book provides nothing short of a spiritual formation within the holy space of biomedical ethics."

—**Allen H. Roberts II**, professor of clinical medicine; chair, Clinical Ethics Committee; affiliate scholar, Pellegrino Center for Clinical Bioethics, Georgetown University Medical Center

"Ben Mitchell's *Bioethics and Medicine* is a uniquely welcomed contribution to the field of Christian bioethics. Focusing more on the 'spirit' and 'attitude' of Christian bioethics than on all the technical issues and controversies, readers will get a wonderful introduction to the heart of Christian bioethics and why we care for the person in the manner we do."

—**Andrew T. Walker**, associate professor of Christian ethics and public theology, The Southern Baptist Theological Seminary; fellow, The Ethics and Public Policy Center

BIOETHICS *and* MEDICINE

ESSENTIALS *in Christian Ethics*

BIOETHICS *and* MEDICINE

A Short Companion

C. Ben Mitchell

editors
C. Ben Mitchell & Jason Thacker

Bioethics and Medicine: A Short Companion

Published by B&H Academic®
Brentwood, Tennessee

ISBN: 978-1-0877-8888-3

Dewey Decimal Classification: 241
Subject Heading: CHRISTIAN ETHICS \
BIOETHICS \ MEDICAL ETHICS

Cover design by Emily Keafer Lambright.
Cover illustration by J614/iStock.

Printed in the United States of America

30 29 28 27 26 25 VP 1 2 3 4 5 6 7 8 9 10

To Dr. Robert L. (Bob) Mounts, who taught me to ask one of life's most important questions: "So what?"

CONTENTS

SERIES PREFACE

In 1876, German Lutheran theologian Christoph Ernst Luthardt eloquently illustrated the relationship between theology and ethics. He wrote, "God first loved us is the summary of Christian doctrine. We love Him is the summary of Christian morality."[1] The wedding of theology and ethics was later embraced by generations of theologians and ethicists, such as Protestant titans Herman Bavinck and Carl F. H. Henry,[2] who rightly understood the primacy of both theology and ethics in the Christian life. But at times in the recent history of the Protestant church, the study of ethics has been relegated to a mere application of theology and biblical studies rather than understood as a first-order discipline in rich partnership with the theological task.

The aim of the Christian ethic can be summed up in the words of Jesus in Matt 22:37–39. We, God's people, are to "love the Lord

---

[1] Christoph Ernst Luthardt, *Apologetic Lectures on the Moral Truths of Christianity*, trans. Sophia Taylor (Edinburgh: T&T Clark, 1876), 26.

[2] See Herman Bavinck, *Reformed Ethics*, ed. John Bolt, vol. 1, *Created, Fallen, and Converted Humanity* (Grand Rapids: Baker, 2019), §1:58; and Carl F. H. Henry, *Christian Personal Ethics*, 2nd ed. (Grand Rapids: Baker, 1979), 486.

[our] God with all [our] heart[s] and with all [our] soul[s] and with all [our] mind[s] . . . and to love [our] neighbor as [ourselves]." We hear echoes of this summation in the words of Luthardt, Bavinck, and Henry, each of whom spoke of how God's people are to love him as the summary of Christian morality. Thus, Christian ethics is nothing less than a primary motivation for those seeking to be faithful to God in all of life and live in light of how he has revealed himself in Scripture. Ethics as discipleship is a key theme throughout Scripture and one the church must elevate as we seek God's face in the academy, in our churches, and especially in our personal lives as transformed creatures made in the very image of God.

While Christian ethics is a core element of God's revelation to his people about how they are to live as his followers, it is also a distinct philosophical discipline that must be studied in consideration of the rich history of moral thought seen throughout the life of the church and the wider society. Much of today's discourse about Christian ethics tends to focus on the mere application of theological or philosophical principles, rather than understanding how these principles have been derived and refined over time in light of the massive metaphysical and epistemological shifts in the history of thought.

Given the recent tendency in wider evangelicalism at times to downplay the direct study of ethics in our curricula, in our church life, and in the task of discipleship, the Essentials in Christian Ethics series is designed to illuminate the richness of the Christian ethic, as well as how ethics is intricately woven into the whole of the Christian life. We have gathered renowned ethicists and leading figures in their fields of theological and philosophical inquiry who are passionate about proclaiming the biblical ethic to a world desperately in need of Christ.

The series is made up of short, introductory volumes spanning metaethics, normative ethics, and applied ethics. Each volume can be used independently as an introduction to the crucial elements of the Christian ethical tradition, including resources for further reading and key concepts for those seeking to dig deeper into the beauty of God's revelation. They can also be used as supplements to a larger ethics curriculum, where a specialized volume could be used to augment a primary text or to give deeper insight into particular contemporary ethical debates.

As editors, we have longed for a series like this to be written by scholars who understand and apply the rich relationship of theology and ethics in their teaching, writings, and ministry. This series is designed to model for readers how the biblical ethic applies to every area of life both as a distinct theological and philosophical discipline in the context of the Christian moral tradition from a robust Protestant viewpoint. We pray this serves the wider academy, those training in our colleges and seminaries, and especially those seeking to employ the riches of Christian ethics in the context of the local church.

C. Ben Mitchell and Jason Thacker
Series Editors

ACKNOWLEDGMENTS

Kentucky essayist, poet, and novelist Wendell Berry has described the inhabitants of his fictional town of Port William as a "membership." They are part of a community. I have been the beneficiary of being kindly invited into a membership. And this book would not have been written without its members.

The first to welcome me was my *doktorvater*, Glenn C. Graber, professor emeritus of philosophy at the University of Tennessee–Knoxville, who, in addition to teaching us a case-based approach to medical ethics, was an excellent guide to the clinical context of medicine, especially the physician-patient relationship. Another individual who welcomed me was Nigel M. de S. Cameron, founding editor of the journal *Ethics and Medicine: An International Journal of Bioethics* and the visionary behind the founding of the Center for Bioethics and Human Dignity.

I owe innumerable physicians a debt of gratitude for their hospitality to a nonphysician. Getting to know one of the shapers of contemporary medical ethics, the late Edmund Pellegrino, MD, was formative in my thinking about medicine, as were the work and influence of Leon Kass, MD, who is one of the most thoughtful, perceptive, and brilliant people I have ever known. Each of these men chaired the President's Council on Bioethics during the George W. Bush presidency, leading the council to produce some of the most salient reflections on biomedicine and biotechnology in history.

Among close personal friends who practice medicine daily, I must mention C. Christopher Hook, MD, and William "Bill" Cheshire, MD, a hematologist and a neurologist, respectively, of Mayo Clinic. Together and separately, we have spent countless hours celebrating and lamenting both the wonder and the profound challenges facing the contemporary practice of medicine and the development of emerging biotechnologies.

The members of the Ethics Committee of the Christian Medical and Dental Associations, chaired by D. Joy Riley, MD, have been an inspiring cadre of faithful physicians with whom to think and learn. I wish every professional thought as deeply about their vocation as do these physicians.

I'm grateful, too, for my coeditor in the Essentials series, Jason Thacker, and the team at B&H Academic, including Madison Trammel, Michael McEwen, and Renée Chavez. The editorial team have been superb partners to work with. And I must mention the warm comradery of the Green Ink Grove Writer's Group in Chattanooga, who gave me very helpful feedback on one section of the book.

Finally, Paul House and Richard Bailey are consistent encouragers to do work that is meaningful and useful.

I don't expect any of these friends to agree with me on everything—perhaps not on anything—but I am indebted to them for the inspiration to think deeply about the practice of medicine as an inherently moral relationship and not just as body plumbing.

C. Ben Mitchell, PhD
Feast of St. Nicholas 2024

INTRODUCTION TO *BIOETHICS AND MEDICINE*

> Medicine is, so to speak, what it does . . . It also requires that medicine is to be seen as an inherently moral enterprise. In as much as it entails the use of power for the benefit of those in need and requires a particular understanding of human flourishing that it seeks to foster, moral questions operate internally to the practice of medicine, rather than being an imposition from external religious or moral systems.
>
> —ANDREW SLOANE, *VULNERABILITY AND CARE*

> O man full of arts, to one it is given to create the things of art, and to another to judge what measure of harm and of profit they have for those that shall employ them.
>
> —SOCRATES, IN PLATO'S *PHAEDRUS*

I am not a doctor, and I do not play one on television. I am a bioethicist by training and credentials. Fifty years ago, few people, if any, would have worn that title. In one real sense—as I am burdened to convince you in this book—bioethics is as old as medicine; at the same time, the area of applied ethics now known as bioethics only emerged after the mid-twentieth century. One of the momentous developments that led to its genesis was a new technology to provide kidney dialysis, raising important questions about access to scarce life-saving resources. There were relatively few dialysis machines for the many potential patients who might benefit from dialysis. So, hospital committees were formed to help facilitate decisions about who would be eligible to receive this vital treatment.

In November 1962, *Life* magazine writer Shana Alexander published an article about one of those committees at Seattle's Swedish Hospital. With the ominous title "The 'God Committee' Deciding Life and Death," the article featured a two-page photo of a committee sitting at a conference table with only their silhouettes visible to readers. No faces could be recognized. Under the photo was the line "They Decide Who Lives, Who Dies" and below that, "Medical Miracle Puts Moral Burden on Small Committee."[1]

The committee was appointed by Seattle's King County Medical Society, which provided no moral or ethical guidelines. The committee included ordinary citizens: a banker, a housewife, an official of state government, a labor leader, a surgeon, and a minister (who was most clearly identifiable by the clerical collar visible in the photograph). In one yearlong period of time, they would essentially determine the fate of five individuals by deciding whether those individuals would get a shot at the limited number of kidney dialysis machines. How would they decide? How could they decide? By what set of criteria? What ethical principles would be followed?

---

[1] Shana Alexander, "They Decide Who Lives, Who Dies: Medical Miracle and a Moral Burden of a Small Committee," *Life*, November 9, 1962, 103–28. See https://www.nephjc.com/news/godpanel.

As historian M. L. Tina Stevens has argued, this issue was only one of a number of pressure points in medicine and the technology of medicine that birthed modern-day bioethics. As she describes it, "The bioethics 'movement' . . . assisted in transforming alarm over exotic technologies into a situation in which ethical experts manage problems—problems generated by technologies seen, ironically, as value-neutral in their creation even while they are problem-causing in their outcomes."[2] We will meet some of these so-called experts and problem-causing technologies in the following chapters, although this is not a book about the history of bioethics. In fact, I want to convince readers that the ethics of medicine is not about experts managing problems but rather about an ancient profession with inherited moral values that guide the practice of medicine and that are at risk of being eviscerated if Christians and others do not intervene.

Contemporary American health care is broken. Just try to get a new primary care physician (PCP) for yourself. It can take long weeks, sometimes months, to get an appointment. When you finally see the doctor, he or she may seem as interested in a digital device as in you as a patient. Make no mistake about it, ticking boxes on the device is not as much about your history and care as it is about compliance with third-party payers such as insurance companies and government agencies like Medicare. And if the doctor is not ticking those boxes, a relative newcomer to patient care, sometimes unintroduced to you, is standing there taking notes. They are called scribes, and their job is to do the digital data gathering for the physician. So now, a different kind of third party has been introduced into a space that was once

[2] M. L. Tina Stevens, *Bioethics in America: Origins and Cultural Politics* (Baltimore: Johns Hopkins University Press, 2000), xiii.

thought to be sacrosanct, as private as the relationship between a priest and parishioner.

The erosion of the physician-patient relationship works the other way too. Physicians become just another cog in the machinery of the medical industrial complex. As one physician put it rather crudely but doubtless accurately, "I have to move, move, move if I want to keep the lights on."[3] If he spends ten minutes with a patient, he can make a profit. If he spends twelve minutes with a patient, he only breaks even. If he spends fourteen or more minutes with a patient, he loses money.

I remember needing a new PCP at one point and calling various "providers" in my insurance network to try to discern whether the physician and I might see eye-to-eye on what I thought were very important medical ethical issues. After all, since I was going to trust my well-being and, potentially, my life to this person, it would seem important that we are compatible. So, I would call a doctor's office and ask to speak to the physician. I was invariably intercepted on the phone by a nurse or office manager. I would explain my reason for calling and ask, "Can you tell me whether Dr. So-and-so approves of physician-assisted suicide or euthanasia?"

Admittedly, this was a rather crude way to begin, but I thought it might save both of us time and effort by not waiting until the first office visit to find that we were not ethically well matched. Almost without exception, whoever I was speaking with would say something like, "Oh, the doctor could not do that because it is illegal." This was obviously before that particular state legalized physician-assisted suicide (PAS). In an increasing number of jurisdictions,

---

[3] Abraham M. Nussbaum, MD, *The Finest Traditions of My Calling: One Physician's Search for the Renewal of Medicine* (New Haven, CT: Yale University Press, 2016), 2.

that rationale could not be offered. But never mind, that was not what I was really trying to get at. What I wanted to learn was the doctor's ethical views, not his or her views about the law. I wanted to know if the doctor had moral scruples about killing patients. That seems a reasonable thing to want to know.

Despite not getting the clarity I had hoped for, I made an appointment with a new doctor. On that first uncomfortable visit, which must be a little bit like speed dating, he asked why I was there. I said, "I need a new PCP, and you are in my network." He looked at me with a Grinch-like stare and replied calmly but insistently, "I did not go to medical school to become a PCP! I went to medical school to practice internal medicine." *Well,* I thought to myself, *although that did not turn out quite as I had wished, at least we are getting somewhere.* He saw his role more as I saw it, not as an agent of the health-care industrial complex but as a medical professional and specialist. I apologized, of course, and we had a quite clarifying conversation about who he was as a physician and who I was as his new patient.

Perhaps your first encounter with a new physician was not with your PCP (now you know not to use those initials except on insurance forms) but was following an emergency room visit that resulted in your admission to the hospital. Instead of your regular physician, who presumably would know you, your recent medical history, your medications, and perhaps any chronic conditions, you were seen by someone with one of the most impersonal—and I would add unprofessional of all titles—a "hospitalist." Instead of the title of their medical specialty (e.g., family medicine, general practice, internal medicine), they wear the title of their location. This person—well-trained, compassionate, and experienced as he or she may be—has never met you before, never examined you before, and knows nothing about you except what can be found in the scanty records created as you were being admitted to that hospital. There are many pros and cons about using hospitalists, but I will argue that it is far from an ideal situation.

If all of this is not sufficient to describe the status quo (which someone once said is Latin for "the mess we're in"), the medical system's brokenness is seen even more clearly upon discharge from the hospital as the bills from the hospital begin arriving. If you are fortunate enough to have health-care insurance, you must first meet a deductible. That is, you must pay a certain amount out of pocket before your insurance company begins to pay. Pages and pages arrive in the mail with lists that appear to be written in a foreign language of tests, procedures, room costs, medical costs, and the like, with almost no itemized lists for you to compare what you were charged for with what you actually used. Do you remember using an "emesis basin"? No worries, you paid for one. And you know that four-inch by four-inch gauze surgical pad that would cost at most a couple of dollars at your local pharmacy? It was eight dollars. Why? Among other things, that is what the insurance will reimburse.

The Future of Medicine

No worries, we are told, the future is bright. Technology will be our savior. As I write, a collaboration of the University of Denver, the National Institutes of Health, the National Science Foundation, and others are developing Robot You Always Needed (RYAN). According to the website, RYAN is "a social companion for aging adults. Research with RYAN has demonstrated his ability to slow cognitive decline, enhance mood, improve memory retention, and more. RYAN is more than just a cutting-edge social robot. He is a friend, assistant, and an unwavering companion" whose features include the following:

Emotional Expression Programming
Chat Using Natural Language Processing
Facial Recognition Software
Serious Brain Games
Physical Activities (Yoga)
Usage and Progress Tracking
Emotional Expression
Cognitive Behavioral Therapy
Automated Speech Recognition[4]

Twenty-first-century physicians will increasingly use artificial intelligence (AI) not just in ways that are already imbedded in our technologies and not just to augment human medicine, but perhaps as a replacement for tasks that have for generations been performed by other human beings. In April 2023, physicians at UC San Diego and the University of Wisconsin began experimenting with ChatGPT technology to help respond to patients' questions. Nidhi Subbaraman reported in the *Wall Street Journal*:

> Marlene Millen, a primary care physician at UC San Diego Health who is helping lead the AI test, has been testing GPT in her inbox for about a week. Early AI-generated responses needed heavy editing, she said, and her team has been working to improve the replies. They are also adding a kind of bedside manner: If a patient mentioned returning from a trip, the draft could include a line that asked if

[4] DreamFace Technologies LLC website, accessed October 14, 2024, https://dreamfacetech.com/.

> their travels went well. "It gives the human touch that we would," Dr. Millen said.[5]

Yes, you read that right: the nonhuman chatbot "gives the human touch that we would." Breathtaking.

These are examples of ethical issues in medicine. Unfortunately, we tend to think of medical ethics as dilemma ethics, where some sort of crisis is to be sorted out or a conundrum is to be resolved. It may be whether abortion is morally permissible if a mother's life is at risk. It may be whether we ought to perform genetic tests on embryos. It may be if or when it is ethical to remove a dying patient from a ventilator. Or it may be, as I queried my would-be PCPs, whether PAS is morally defensible. There is almost an infinite number of possible scenarios that present themselves in health care. They are real, and they often make the news and land in the courts.

But these are not the issues I deal with in this book, at least directly. Rather, I will try to describe what I believe is the normative ethical relationship between a physician and his or her patient. I also will outline what I, and others, understand to be the relationship between human health in a tragically fallen world of disease and death and the care of strangers. And I will tackle some of the technological questions that are currently emerging, such as whether Carebots like RYAN really care and whether their use is consistent with the ethical demands of human medicine. In short, my aim is to rehydrate a conception of Christian Hippocratic medicine. More about that in the first chapter.

---

[5] Nidhi Subbaraman, "ChatGPT Will See You Now: Doctors Using AI to Answer Patient Questions," *Wall Street Journal*, April 28, 2023. Also available at https://www.wsj.com/articles/dr-chatgpt-physicians-are-sending-patients-advice-using-ai-945cf60b.

Our Journey Together

I must state here at the beginning of our journey, however, that I have both a seminary degree and a doctoral degree in philosophy with a concentration in medical ethics. I chose that educational trajectory because I sensed a call to serve the church as a pastor. It was in that pastoral context that profound ethical issues arose. First was the experience my wife and I had with infertility. Although it was early in the evolution of artificial reproductive technology, we both felt the desire to have children and were offered the maze of options that were available to couples in our situation. We will talk about some of these later in the book.

At the other end of life, deeply troubled church members were telling me, "The doctor says it is time to take Granny off the ventilator. Pastor, what should we do?" At that time I had no meaningful resources to draw on. I was a young pastor, and my seminary training did not cover end-of-life issues. We had two class periods to debate the pros and cons of euthanasia in my ethics class, so I was pretty sure what we should not do. We should not kill Granny. But I was not taught how, much less what, to think theologically and pastorally about end-of-life care.

So I discovered, much to my delight, that a couple of hours from where I was serving there was a doctoral program in philosophy that included a concentration in medical ethics. What that meant for me was that I would do all the coursework, papers, and exams for a rigorous degree in the history of philosophy and ethical theory, but my focus would be applied ethics. I would have advanced seminars in medical ethics, clinical ethics, mental health ethics, genetic ethics, justice, and other subjects. I would take a course in medical terminology. But the *pièce de résistance* was that my program required that I have real-life, in-hospital clinical training in the form of clinical rounds. For one academic year I would show up at a tertiary-care teaching hospital in the wee hours of the morning to do rounds with attending physicians, medical residents, medical students, social workers, pharmacists, chaplains, and others. I wore a white pressed cotton lab coat with "Medical Ethics" embroidered over the left chest pocket, had a hospital name badge dangling from my lapel, and was required to do rounds in most of the services of the hospital. I was in the alphabet soup of the CCU, NICU, PICU, and MICU.

During those rounds I did things such as following a kidney transplant from beginning to end. On one occasion, I met the patient and the family donor and discussed with them their understanding of the procedure and its risks. The next morning, I donned pale blue hospital scrubs—the uniform of the hospital culture—scrubbed in as if I were going to be doing the surgery myself and, with outstretched arms, received sterile nitrile gloves from an operating room technician. Once under the blazing light of the operating room, with the surgeon's favorite music playing softly in the background, I stood on a stainless-steel stool above the transplant team peering down into both patients' bodies. Serious conversation about the procedure was dotted with the occasional pun or quip. The deftness of the surgeon and his colleagues was mesmerizing, despite frequent whiffs of cauterizing human flesh.

On another occasion, I spent a late night in a surgical suite with a team from the state donor services organization observing the retrieval of tissues and organs from four teenagers who had been killed in a car wreck that night. Although most physicians and nurses approve of organ donation, that evening the donor services team confessed to me outside the surgical suite that they had a hard time being in the vicinity of organ retrieval from the newly deceased. The emotional weight of dissecting tissues and organs from four high schoolers was just too hard to bear. Although necessary, respectful, and appropriate, it still felt macabre.

On another clinical rotation, I vividly recall spending night after night in the emergency department (ED) shadowing an emergency physician. That is when I learned that the ED is best described by that almost palpable definition of flying as "hours and hours of boredom, punctuated by brief moments of stark terror." The doctor would take me with him into the examination room and say to the patient or family, "This is Ben; he is a medical ethics doctoral student. Is it okay if he joins us?" Whether or not they knew what medical ethics was, not a single person declined. After all, I had on a white lab coat just like the others. I must be okay.

Many Friday and Saturday nights, I would hope against hope to see something interesting. I was a student, after all. I was there to learn something I could write up in a case report describing what I had observed each evening. More often than not, it was just one sniffling little kid after another. But then, just when things would get quiet, an alarm would sound in the ED, and a phone would ring to alert the team that the Life Flight helicopter was bringing in a patient. The team in the air would rattle off a brief description of the patient, the extent of the injury, and the patient's vital signs. In the ED, it was everyone to their battle stations, as it were. I was allowed to stand against the wall, voyeur-like, to watch a well-caffeinated, adrenaline-pumped medical team attempt sometimes heroic feats to save human lives.

Either the doctor or one of the ED nurses would always invite me in but, at the same time, warn me with unmistakable seriousness, "If you start to feel faint, get the hell out of here. We do not need another patient to treat!" Despite seeing a few grisly things, only on one occasion did that become a problem. They rushed a man into the emergency bay trailed by a phalanx of nurses, residents, and finally the attending emergency physician. As each member of the team was following the well-rehearsed choreography of care, I watched as a nurse inserted a peripheral venous catheter into the top of the man's hand. He let out a bloodcurdling scream when she pushed that needle into his vein. Somehow, I subconsciously identified with him at that moment. I began to feel my vision growing darker, and cold sweat formed on my temples and neck. My stomach got queasy, and I knew that if I remained there, I was going to pass out and that, even if I did not get injured in the fall, the head nurse was going to kick my butt. So without saying a word, I slipped out of the room, finding the quickest door to the outside where the night air was crisp and dry. Leaning against the handrail, taking deep breaths, I recovered from my near-fatal encounter with an angry health-care professional and slipped back into the room. I suspect that my departure and arrival were noticed—they do not miss much in those rooms—but no one mentioned it, perhaps just to spare me the embarrassment.

In addition to the year-long medical rounds, we were required to spend a summer at the state in-patient mental health hospital exploring and observing the issues that arise in mental health ethics. Questions about the care of incompetent patients, the use of chemical straitjackets, and the role of the state in protecting individuals who are considered a harm to themselves and to others hung in the air like the summer humidity.

Where Are We Going?

In this book, we will first look at the ancient origins of medicine and medical ethics enshrined in the Hippocratic Oath and its long tradition in medicine. We will spend time thinking about the relationship between a physician and a patient. I aim to convince you that the relationship is more like a covenant than a contract, that patients are persons and not problems to be solved.

We will think about health and health care in the context of a fallen world where disease and death are universal. We will explore ethics at the edges of life—at the beginning of life and at the end of life. What we think about unborn humans before they have developed certain biological and cognitive capacities has implications for what we think about people at the end of life after they have lost certain biological and cognitive capacities.

This journey will take us into the human gene pool. We will think about genetic engineering, genetic enhancement, and the problem of eugenics. Finally, with other friends and colleagues, I will suggest some ways of recovering, reforming, and reimagining the art and science of medicine for a truly human future.

It is a short book, so it will be a bit of a whirlwind. I am glad you are joining me on this journey.

1

The Hippocratic Oath and the Origins of Medical Ethics

> Then the King will say to those on his right, "Come, you who are blessed by my Father; inherit the kingdom prepared for you from the foundation of the world. For I was hungry and you gave me something to eat; I was thirsty and you gave me something to drink; I was a stranger and you took me in; I was naked and you clothed me; I was sick and you took care of me; I was in prison and you visited me."
>
> —Matthew 25:34–36

Western medicine traces its origins to Hippocrates of Kos in the fourth century BC. Sometimes called "the father of medicine," Hippocrates was a Greek physician who founded both a school of medicine and what eventually became a profession with a rich tradition that survives today but is under intense pressure. Most people have heard of Hippocrates because of the oath that bears his name.

Contemporary, cutting-edge, high-technology medicine is a legatee of the Hippocratic tradition and is in many ways still shaped by it, including its moral principles. I will argue in this volume that it ought to be the case that many of the enduring values of the Hippocratic legacy, refracted through the lens of the Christian tradition, should continue to inform and guide contemporary medical ethics.

This chapter recounts those ancient origins. From its beginning, medicine has been a profoundly moral enterprise. Existentially, the relationship between the healer and the vulnerable is morally freighted. Historically, because of their affirmation that every human being is made in the image of God, their commitment to follow Jesus the healer, and the call to love one's neighbor as oneself, Christians have been at the forefront of the care of strangers in the medical context.

The Classic Hippocratic Oath

The first known reference to the Hippocratic Oath is in the work of a medical writer, Scribonius Largus, who lived during the reign of the Roman emperor Claudius (AD 41–54). Scribonius refers to Hippocrates as "the founder of our profession."[1] Those who studied in the school of Hippocrates learned from their teachers—or masters, as they were called—a holistic form of medical practice that viewed patients as vulnerable persons rather than as projects, problems, or profit. The practice of these students—and thus their

[1] See W. H. S. Jones, *The Doctor's Oath: An Essay in the History of Medicine* (Cambridge: Cambridge University Press, 1924), 39.

character—was shaped by an apprenticeship, professional obligations, duties to patients, and bedside observation. Here is the Hippocratic Oath:

> I swear by Apollo the physician, and Aesculapius the surgeon, likewise Hygeia and Panacea, and call all the gods and goddesses to witness, that I will observe and keep this underwritten oath, to the utmost of my power and judgment.
>
> I will reverence my master who taught me the art. Equally with my parents, will I allow him things necessary for his support, and will consider his sons as brothers. I will teach them my art without reward or agreement; and I will impart all my acquirement, instructions, and whatever I know, to my master's children, as to my own; and likewise to all my pupils, who shall bind and tie themselves by a professional oath, but to none else.
>
> With regard to healing the sick, I will devise and order for them the best diet, according to my judgment and means; and I will take care that they suffer no hurt or damage. Nor shall any man's entreaty prevail upon me to administer poison to anyone; neither will I counsel any man to do so. Moreover, I will give no sort of medicine to any pregnant woman, with a view to destroy the child. But in purity and holiness I will guard my life and my art.
>
> Further, I will comport myself and use my knowledge in a godly manner.
>
> I will not cut for the stone, but will commit that affair entirely to the surgeons.
>
> Whatsoever house I may enter, my visit shall be for the convenience and advantage of the patient; and I will

willingly refrain from doing any injury or wrong from falsehood, and (in an especial manner) from acts of an amorous nature, whatever may be the rank of those who it may be my duty to cure, whether mistress or servant, bond or free.

Whatever, in the course of my practice, I may see or hear (even when not invited), whatever I may happen to obtain knowledge of, if it be not proper to repeat it, I will keep sacred and secret within my own breast.

If I faithfully observe this oath, may I thrive and prosper in my fortune and profession, and live in the estimation of posterity; or on breach thereof, may the reverse be my fate![2]

Four Aspects of the Oath

Covenant

Several important features are evident from the Oath. First, the Oath is covenantal. That is, it recognizes the authority of the divine within a covenantal relationship. Although the original Oath is polytheistic, one of its most profound aspects is that it recognizes that the physician's relationship is in a triadic relationship: physician, patient, and deity. That is, it is a pledge or promise made before the divine, where the responsibilities undertaken in the relationship between the physician and patient are sanctioned by the gods (or in Christian theology, by the one God). This is a striking

[2] "Hippocratic Oath—Classic," McCollough Scholars: Pre-Medical Studies at the University of Alabama, accessed October 14, 2024, https://mccolloughscholars.as.ua.edu/hippocratic-oath-classic/.

acknowledgment against the backdrop of today's secularization of medicine. The third person in this covenantal relationship between the deity and the physician is the patient. As Nigel M. de S. Cameron points out:

> The society in which the Hippocratic Oath was first sworn was profoundly pluralistic, and that was the context in which the Oath invited the physician to commit himself to one particular set of values. His answer to pluralism did not lie in relativizing his own moral and professional commitments and seeking to adapt them to those of his patients. Indeed, the whole purpose of the Oath was to meet the challenge of a plurality of religions and ethical convictions by calling on the physician to assert and practice one particular option among the many.[3]

Duties to Teacher

Second, the Oath acknowledges the debt to others for the art and skill of medicine, especially the teacher with whom the student apprenticed. In fact, the indebtedness is like that of a child to a parent. Not only that but, because of the depth of the relationship, there is a commitment to care for one's teacher that extends to the binding responsibility to pass on the knowledge and art of medicine to one's own pupils. This is a reminder that entering medicine during this period was like entering a guild or craft with its reservoir of art and skill at the disposal of those who practiced it. Contemporary medicine and medical education stand on the

---

[3] Nigel M. de S. Cameron, *The New Medicine: Life and Death After Hippocrates* (Wheaton, IL: Crossway, 1991), 28–29.

shoulders of generations of scientists and practitioners who have gone before those who are being trained today. Physicians are to faithfully pass on their knowledge, skills, wisdom, and practices to the next generation *ad infinitum*.

Duties to Patients

Third, and even more important perhaps, are the duties to patients. The Oath binds those who swear it to use their skills for the good of the patient. The primary duty is to benefit the patients and not to harm them, "that they suffer no hurt or damage." One may often hear it said that the first principle of medical ethics is *primum non nocere* (first, do no harm). Although there is a certain logic behind this assertion, in fact, the duty of beneficence (do good) is at least parallel if not prior to the duty not to harm. The patient's well-being is the heart of medicine's patient-centered approach.

What kinds of harm was Hippocrates envisioning? Although the Oath is generalizable so that all harms are prohibited, it does offer some interesting detail. For instance, despite a patient's wishes, the Hippocratic physician will not participate in assisted suicide by prescribing a life-ending poison. The physician has a better way and will not even suggest such an assault on the dignity of the patient. Nor will the physician provide a pessary (i.e., an abortion-causing intervention) to a woman. To do so, the Oath maintains, would be to violate the purity and holiness of the physician's life and art.

Likewise, the ethical physician will not offer treatments that are outside his or her expertise. Since, at that time, physicians were not trained as surgeons, the Hippocratic physician would not perform surgery or "cut for a stone." Those skills were beyond the scope of practice or the competency of what we might now call a general practitioner. Interestingly, as far back as 2000 BC, what we would call medical malpractice was both identified and punishable. The ancient code of law, the Code of Hammurabi, etched on an obelisk that now resides in the Louvre, includes a reparation for malpractice: "If a surgeon performs a major operation on an 'awelum' (nobleman) with a lancet and caused the death of this man, they shall cut off his hands."[4] Knowing one's appropriate limits—or, in medicine, one's scope of practice—was an important part of the ethical practice of medicine.

Sanctions

One of the indispensable elements of a profession versus an occupation, historically speaking, is that the profession is self-regulating. That is, the members of the professional group—originally, in clergy, law, and medicine—establish the requirements for the profession and hold one another accountable to ethical practice. Positive sanctions are mentioned in the Oath: "If I faithfully observe this oath, may I thrive and prosper in my fortune and profession, and live in the estimation of posterity."

There are also negative sanctions. Within the professional guild, when information about some misbehavior came to light, physicians would often get a "talking-to" by another colleague.[5] In some cases where the infraction was sufficiently egregious, one could be banned from the practice of medicine all together. The negative sanction of the Oath is particularly stark when the physician

---

[4] Tharwat Mohammed Halwani and Mohamad Said Maani Takrouri, "Medical Laws and Ethics of Babylon as Read in Hammurabi's Code," *Internet Journal of Law, Healthcare and Ethics* 4, no 2. Also available at https://ispub.com/IJLHE/4/2/10352.

[5] See Eliot Freidson, *Profession of Medicine: A Study of the Sociology of Applied Knowledge* (Chicago: University of Chicago Press, 1988), 149.

commits himself to the penalty that "on breach thereof, may the reverse be my fate!" The Oath and oath-making of a professional carried a different kind of gravitas than that of another occupation. After all, as physician Farr Curlin and philosopher Chris Tollefsen point out, "Medical practice is neither a pastime nor merely a career; it is a *profession*, whose members make life-shaping commitments to care for particular vulnerable persons."[6] Or as historian of bioethics Albert R. Jonsen puts it, "Medical ethics was incarnate in their [physicians] behavior and character and in the social arrangements that sustained the solidarity, respectability, and educated competence of the profession."[7] This was no less true of the Christian version of the Oath, dating to the second or third century AD.[8]

The Christian Version of the Oath

> Blessed be God the Father of our Lord Jesus Christ, be blessed for ever and ever. I do not lie.
>
> I will not tarnish the science of medicine.
>
> I will not give anyone poison, even if he asks me for it, nor will I suggest anyone to take it.
>
> Likewise, I will not induce abortion in any woman with treatment from above or below.

---

[6] Farr Curlin and Christopher Tollefsen, *The Way of Medicine, Ethics and the Healing Profession* (Notre Dame, IN: University of Notre Dame Press, 2021). Also available at https://www.sweetstudy.com/files/thewayofmedicineethicsandthehealing-pdf.

[7] Albert R. Jonsen, *The Birth of Bioethics* (Oxford: Oxford University Press, 1998), 5.

[8] Jones, *Doctor's Oath*, 22–25.

I will teach the art to those who want to learn it, without hiding anything from them and without making them my servants.

According to my ability and judgement, I will only apply my treatments for the benefit of the sick. I will practice my art with purity and holiness.

In whatever house I enter, I shall enter to help the sick, and I shall refrain from any action, intentional or unintentional, that may cause harm or death, and from any erotic intercourse with servant or free, male or female.

I will keep silent about everything I see or hear, on the occasion of my internship (or even outside of it in my social relations), and I will consider these things as a sacred secret.

If I keep this oath and do not break it, may God help me in my life and in my art, and may I be honoured of men. If I remain faithful, may I be saved; but if I swear falsely, may the contrary befall me.[9]

The Oath Today

How do things stand with the Hippocratic Oath and the profession of medicine today? According to the late former US Surgeon General C. Everett Koop, "In the post-WWII era physicians began

[9] "Christian Hippocratic Oath," Universidad de Navarra website, accessed October 14, 2024, https://en.unav.edu/web/humanities-and-medical-ethics-unit/bioethics-material/juramento-hipocratico-cristiano#gsc.tab=0.

to water down the basic tenets of the Hippocratic tradition, and they abandoned them."[10]

Evidence of the watering down, if not abandonment, of those tenets was seen in a benchmark survey of US medical schools in the mid-1990s by R. D. Orr and others who queried 157 medical schools to discover if they still used the Oath. They found the following:

1 school used the original Oath
68 schools used some version of the Oath
8 percent included the prohibition against abortion
14 percent prohibited euthanasia and assisted suicide
43 percent included some notion of MD accountability
3 percent forbade sexual contact with patients[11]

Comparing these findings with the substance of the original Oath, one may conclude that the Oath may be experiencing, metaphorically speaking, a failure to thrive. More recently, in a study published in the *Archives of Internal Medicine* in 2011, researchers found that the Oath may have a longer shelf life than the earlier survey revealed but that the Oath nevertheless is not universally embraced.

Of 1,032 physicians who returned surveys, 79 percent reported that their medical school conducted an oath ceremony. Of those who took an oath in medical school, 85 percent recall using some version of the Hippocratic Oath, although a few took an Osteopathic Oath, a version of the Prayer of Maimonides, or the Declaration of Geneva. About a quarter of the physicians indicated that the

---

[10] Cameron, *New Medicine*, back cover.

[11] R. D. Orr et al., "Use of the Hippocratic Oath: A Review of Twentieth Century Practice and a Content Analysis of Oaths Administered in Medical Schools in the US and Canada in 1993," *Journal of Clinical Ethics* 8, no. 4 (1997): 377–88.

oath exerted "a lot" of influence on their practice. The remainder reported that the oaths had influence their practice either "somewhat," "not very much," or "not at all."[12]

When asked about other sources of moral guidance in their professional practice, 92 percent said their personal sense of right and wrong was most important, followed by great moral teachers (35 percent), and specific traditions (28 percent). The report concluded, among other things, that "for moral guidance in their professional practice, physicians appear to rely most on their own personal sense of right and wrong with some awareness of the influence of great moral teachers and specific traditions."[13]

It is not that physicians are acting immorally because they do not take the Oath that has shaped the profession down the ages. In most polls, physicians still rank first or second among trusted professionals. A "personal sense of right and wrong," however, is a far cry from the ethical ideals of the professional community enshrined in the Hippocratic Oath. But the reality is that without the formative influence of robust objective ethical commitments, the profession has changed, and not necessarily for the better.

Recovering Christian-Hippocratic Professionalism

Although they did not embrace the polytheism of the original Oath, early Christians saw the common-grace wisdom of the Oath

---

[12] Ryan M. Antiel et al., "The Impact of Medical School Oaths and Other Professional Codes of Ethics: Results of a National Physician Survey," *Archives of Internal Medicine* 171, no. 5 (March 14, 2011): 469–71, https://doi.org/10.1001/archinternmed.2011.47.

[13] Antiel et al., 470.

and appropriated it for themselves "so that a Christian may take it."[14] Two ancient copies of the Christianized oath were even written in the shape of a cross. Jones maintains that the Christian oath not only omits references to pagan deities but also "makes more definite and explicit the promise not to produce abortion."[15] "The relief of pain and suffering," notes Jones of the Christian oath, "should be tied by no fetters and hindered by no trade-union rules. Christian benevolence should be universal."[16] Christians were also in general agreement with the proto-professionalism of the Oath and embraced most of its contours. As Guenter B. Risse has documented in *Mending Bodies, Saving Souls*, his monumental study of the history of hospitals, "Early Christian theology readily accepted the role of medicine in charitable works."[17] We will discuss this in the next chapter.

While most people may agree that physicians are professionals, professionalism has been truncated. "Professional" is a badge everyone wants to wear. And an internet search of professionalism reveals more about etiquette and dress codes than ethical codes and moral standards of a guild. Happily, in my view, there are efforts underway today to revive the standards of professionalism in medicine. One of those efforts is the Medical Professionalism Project. Most of the principles of that project are consistent with Christian-Hippocratic medicine. The preamble of the "The Physician Charter" leads with the claim that "professionalism is the basis of medicine's contract

---

[14] Jones, *Doctor's Oath*, 51.

[15] Jones, 52.

[16] Jones, 54–55.

[17] Guenter B. Risse, *Mending Bodies, Saving Souls: A History of Hospitals* (Oxford: Oxford University Press, 1999), 76.

with society."[18] The charter identifies three primary principles: patient welfare, patient autonomy, and social justice. These are followed by ten commitments.

The first principle, the "principle of primacy of patient welfare," is built on the premise that "altruism contributes to the trust that is central to the physician-patient relationship."[19] In Christian-Hippocratic terms, whether acknowledged or not, medical professionalism is rooted in two broad warrants. The first warrant is Jesus's ministry of healing. Followers of the Great Physician engage in healing ministries because of his example. The second warrant is the Great Commandment to "love the Lord your God with all your heart, with all your soul, with all your mind, and with all your strength. The second is, Love your neighbor as yourself" (Mark 12:30–31). Neighbor love extends Jesus's healing ministry to those who are experiencing illness and "*dis*-ease." Physicians have been granted a unique trust in the Western tradition to provide that kind of care as trusted professionals.

Trust is hard to earn, but easy to lose. As a patient, I need to have confidence that my physician is guided not just by a "personal sense of what is right and wrong" but also by a robust set of ethical ideals. Therefore, physicians and others involved in medical care must hold themselves to the highest ethical standards to maintain that trust in their medical care of patients. So long as medicine continues to earn this trust, society should respect physicians as professionals, not mere providers. The moniker "health-care provider," like the acronym "PCP," undermines the professionalism of

[18] ABIM Foundation, with the ACP Foundation and the European Federation of Internal Medicine, "The Physician Charter," 2002, ABIM Foundation, https://abimfoundation.org/what-we-do/physician-charter.

[19] ABIM Foundation et al., "The Physician Charter."

medicine and has led to many of the pathologies of contemporary health care.

Without the kind of objective ethical standards of Christian-Hippocratic professionalism, medicine will continue to become just another of the consumer goods of our society and will eventually lose its way. In the words of Curlin and Tollefsen, it will become "something amorphous, subjective, and shadowy."[20] What they describe as the "provider of services" model of medicine values the physician-patient relationship in "terms of economic exchange" (i.e., consumerism) rather than being grounded in the professional altruism of Christian-Hippocratism.

The next chapter will outline the place of the patient as a person in medicine. Chapter 3 will discuss more about the relationship between patient and physician. As Cruess and Cruess put it, "Every physician during his or her practice simultaneously fills two roles—that of the healer and of the professional."[21] What I will attempt to demonstrate is that that association is not like the contractual connection between a provider and a consumer but is rather a very different kind of relationship, a covenantal relationship between persons.

---

[20] Curlin and Tollefsen, *Way of Medicine*, i–ii.

[21] Sylvia Cruess and Richard L. Cruess, "Professionalism and the Social Contract," in *Healing as Vocation: A Medical Professionalism Primer*, ed. Kayhan P. Parsi and Miles Sheehan (Lanham, MD: Roman & Littlefield, 2006), 11.

2

The Patient as Person and the Goals of Medicine

Just as a man is a *sacredness in the social and political order*, so he is a *sacredness in the natural, biological order*. He is a sacredness in bodily life. He is a person who within the ambience of the flesh claims our care. He is an embodied soul or ensouled body. He is therefore a sacredness in illness and in his dying. He is a sacredness in the fruits of the generative processes. . . . The sanctity of human life prevents ultimate trespass upon him even for the sake of treating his bodily life, or for the sake of others who are also only a sacredness in their bodily lives.

—Paul Ramsey, Preface to *The Patient as Person*

Christianity is almost the only one of the great religions which thoroughly approves of the body—which believes that matter is good, that God Himself once took on a human body, that some kind of body is going to be given to us even in Heaven and is going to be an essential part of our happiness, our beauty, and our energy.

—C. S. Lewis, *Mere Christianity*

If the Hippocratic tradition represents the first incarnation of medical ethics, the work of Paul Ramsey represents the contemporary incarnation of medical ethics. During his career as a professor at Princeton University, Ramsey was among others who helped provide the architecture of medical ethics as we know it today. Although he wrote on a range of topics, his *magnum opus* in medical ethics is his Lyman Beecher Lectures at Yale University, published in 1970 as *The Patient as Person: Explorations in Medical Ethics*, followed closely by his Bampton Lectures, published a decade later as *Ethics at the Edges of Life: Medical and Legal Intersections*.

The problems of medical ethics are especially urgent in modern times, and in his preface to *The Patient as Person*, Ramsey fires a formidable opening salvo:

> These are by no means technical problems on which only the expert (in this case, the physician) can have an opinion. They are rather the problems of human beings in situations in which medical care is needed. Birth and death, illness and injury are not simply events the doctor attends. They are moments in every human life. The doctor makes decisions as an expert but also as a man among men; and his patient is a human being coming to his birth or to his death, or being rescued from illness or injury in between.[1]

According to Ramsey, then, medical ethics is not only the purview of medical professionals but is also within the scope of

[1] Paul Ramsey, Albert R. Jonsen, and William F. May, *The Patient as Person: Explorations in Medical Ethics* (New Haven, CT: Yale University Press, 1970), xliv.

those most affected by illness or injury: patients themselves. By definition, a patient is a "sufferer." Patients are not "clients" or "customers"; they are those suffering from illness or "dis-ease" caused by something going awry in their psychophysiology.

At the same time, Ramsey calls on physicians to "become moral philosophers, asking themselves some quite profound questions about the nature of proper moral reasoning, and how moral dilemmas are rightly to be resolved. If they do not, the existing medical ethics will be eroded more and more by what it is alleged *must* be done and technically can be done."[2] Physicians are not body plumbers or technicians. They are moral agents providing a profoundly vital ministry for those who are often suffering "the slings and arrows of outrageous fortune," to quote The Bard.[3] As Tyler Tate and Joseph Clair put it more recently, "For a clinician to act morally, they must first learn to be moral, a difficult process that must be enacted and reenacted throughout one's training and professional life."[4]

In her insightful work *Medicine as Ministry: Reflections on Suffering, Ethics, and Hope*, physician Margaret E. Mohrmann reminds us that patients are persons to whom "a terrible thing is happening and, whatever other name this terrible thing bears, its name is tragedy."[5] This fact helps to provide the clue to answering

---

[2] Ramsey, Jonsen, and May, xlviii. Emphasis original.

[3] William Shakespeare, *Hamlet*, 3.1.58. References are to act, scene, and line.

[4] Tyler Tate and Joseph Clair, "Love Your Patient as Yourself: On Reviving the Broken Heart of American Medical Ethics," *Hastings Center Report* (March–April 2023): 20.

[5] Margaret E. Mohrmann, *Medicine as Ministry: Reflections on Suffering, Ethics, and Hope* (Cleveland, OH: Pilgrim, 1995), 69.

the question, What is medicine for? Or, perhaps better, Who is medicine for?

Recovering the Human Being in Medicine

One of the challenges of contemporary medicine is the potential to objectify or altogether lose the person who is ill. Patients are increasingly identified by their insurance carrier, Medicare or Medicaid number, a treatment bay in the ED, a room on a hospital corridor, or a diagnosis. She is the Medicaid patient with metastatic breast cancer in Room 3-B, instead of Mary, the wife of Bryan, mother of three children, who is hoping against hope that she will live long enough to see her eldest get married, her middle child graduate from high school, and her youngest from middle school. Keeping the patient as person in sharp relief is challenging in contemporary medical practice. This is somewhat paradoxical since if there were no patients there would be no need of medicine. Furthermore, this reality is another reminder that medical ethics is not only, or even primarily, about thorny ethical and legal dilemmas but about rightly ordering the aims of medicine in a close relationship with this or that particular person who is suffering.

Veatch's Four Models

In a benchmark essay on the physician-patient relationship, Robert Veatch, one of the founding figures in contemporary bioethics, explored several ways of looking at that relationship, each of which offers a different characterization of the patient and the aims of medicine.

The Engineering Model

The first model is called the engineering model. In this model the physician is an applied scientist, and the patient is the subject of the scientific method. Looking for significant "facts," "data," and "lab results" answers the question, What should be done? Rather than establishing the patient's values, aims, and desires, the physician-scientist applies the powers of science to diagnose and treat. Physicians become more like engineers making repairs, plumbers flushing clogged systems, or mechanics connecting various parts to other parts. The patient is merely the location of the needed repairs.

The Priestly Model

The second model is what Veatch calls the priestly model. Where once men in white collars and vestments with crosses hanging from their necks functioned as priests in the culture, now men and women in the vestments of white lab coats with stethoscopes around their necks function in a priestly capacity. The physician's office or the hospital room is the sanctuary, and a priestly paternalism characterizes the relationship. The priestly model leads to what Veatch describes as "as-a syndrome." For example, in counseling a pregnant woman who is carrying a child who has been exposed *in utero* to thalidomide, "a physician says, 'The odds are against a normal baby, and speaking as a physician that is a risk you shouldn't take.'"[6] "Speaking as a physician" is code for "I know what is best." This is the problem of generalization of expertise. The patient is more of a parishioner who comes to the priest for confirmation,

---

[6] Robert M. Veatch, *The Patient-Physician Relation: The Patient as Partner, Part 2* (Bloomington: Indiana University Press, 1991), 12.

absolution, and rules for decision-making than a moral agent with values and goals she brings into the relationship herself.

The Collegial Model

The collegial model is Veatch's third way of understanding the relationship between a physician and patient. The physician is the patient's "pal." When two or more are truly committed to common goals, then trust, confidence, and collegiality may result. But especially in our pluralistic culture, there is no guarantee that the physician and the patient share common goals, much less share confidence in the means to accomplish those goals. The Jehovah's Witness with acute anemia, for instance, may wish for his condition to improve, but he will not submit to his "buddy's" remedy of a blood transfusion. This kind of collegiality, opines Veatch, is too utopian for realistic medicine.

The Contractual Model

Finally, Veatch points to the contractual model as another way of understanding the relationship between patients and their physicians. In this model two individuals or groups interact in ways where there are obligations and expected benefits for both parties. The relationship is a quid pro quo (this for that) exchange. Patients bring certain goods and expectations into the relationship, such as the ability to pay for services. Likewise, physicians bring certain goods and expectations into the relationship, such as the skills and tools to provide those services.[7] Although Veatch suggests

[7] Robert Veatch, "Models for Ethical Medicine in a Revolutionary Age," *Hastings Center Report* 2, no. 3 (June 1972): 5–7. For a similar

that "the notion of contract should not be loaded with legalistic implications,"[8] I will attempt to show in the next chapter that this is exactly what has happened. Consumerism, with its pathologies, has made medicine just legalistic enough for the courts and too legalistic for real people, both physicians and patients.

The Healing and Flourishing Model of Who Medicine Is For

Seeing physicians as healers and the aim of medicine as human flourishing is a richer, fuller, and more promising model of the physician-patient relationship. The word "physician" is from the Latin *phiske,* pointing to a person skilled in the art of healing. The goal of medicine is for the suffering patient to flourish as well as he or she is realistically able to under the circumstances. This way of understanding the goals of medicine requires a deep theological foundation.

In his extraordinary volume *Flourishing: Health, Disease, and Bioethics in Theological Perspective*, Neil Messer offers an architecture for understanding the role of medicine in the context of the human condition. The foundation is built, as it were, on a number of important pillars, which are discussed in the remainder of this chapter.

Embodiment

Messer begins by affirming the creatureliness of human beings: "A theological account of health and disease must begin by recognizing

analysis, see Ezekiel J. Emanuel and Linda L. Emanuel, "Four Models of the Physician-Patient Relationship," *JAMA* 267 (1992): 2221–26.

[8] Veatch, *Patient-Physician Relation*, 14.

that we are creatures of a particular kind; what this means, we understand theologically in light of Jesus Christ. As creatures of a particular kind, human beings have both proximate and ultimate ends, which are God's gifts to us in creating us beings of this kind. Our good or flourishing consists in the fulfillment of these ends."[9]

Messer makes the important point that Christology—our way of understanding the person and nature of the God-man, Jesus Christ—is the best lens through which to understand anthropology, the nature of human persons. In the humanity of Jesus, we clearly see certain features of our nature as embodied creatures. "To understand health theologically," Messer maintains, "we must understand what it means to be a creature *of this particular kind*."[10] Although we will say more about this later, let us say that from the incarnation of Christ we see that to be human is, first, to be an embodied member of the species *Homo sapiens*. We are creatures with physical bodies and all that those bodies require to maintain homeostasis (biological stability). Hence, some of the first classes physicians take in medical training are human gross anatomy and physiology. To understand illness and disease, it is necessary to understand how the human body works and what it means for the body to function normally.

Although much in contemporary Christianity tends to lean toward a Gnostic view of human beings[11]—treating the spiritual as more important than the physical—medicine cannot afford that luxury (nor can Christianity, truth be told). It is true, as Messer contends,

---

[9] Neil Messer, *Flourishing: Health, Disease, and Bioethics in Theological Perspective* (Grand Rapids: Eerdmans, 2013), 164.

[10] Messer, 164–65.

[11] See Phillip J. Lee, *Against the Protestant Gnostics* (Oxford: Oxford University Press, 1993); Peter R. Jones, *The Gnostic Empire Strikes Back: An Old Heresy for the New Age* (Phillipsburg, NJ: P&R, 1992).

that "our ultimate end is life in union with God,"[12] but what he calls the proximate (this-worldly) ends are equally important. We are not only bodies, we are souls; but we are not less than bodies. We are ensouled bodies or embodied souls. Embodiment matters.

So, he says, "There are penultimate or proximate ends that are both objective and universal, given simply by virtue of our being creatures of this particular, human, kind. Knowledge of these ends comes in the first place from God's revelation in Christ, rather than any empirical study of the human species, but many kinds of human knowledge and insight can be critically assimilated to this theological understanding."[13]

The Limited, Dependent, Relational Nature of Humanity

Like Jesus the Messiah, the second person of the Trinity, all human beings are not only embodied but also limited, dependent, and relational.[14] Although we are tempted to think of these aspects of our humanity as burdens, they are the gifts of our created humanity. This is what it means to be human. Our bodies are limited in time and space. We are finite in strength, intelligence, and memory. We depend on God. As Paul declared on Mars Hill, "In him we live and move and have our being, as even some of your own poets have said, 'For we are also his offspring'" (Acts 17:28). We are dependent

---

[12] Messer, *Flourishing*, 168.

[13] Messer, 201.

[14] Although there is not space here to unpack everything that this means, readers will find a great deal of very practical help in Kelly M. Kapic, *You're Only Human: How Your Limits Reflect God's Design and Why That's Good News* (Ada, MI: Brazos, 2022); Gilbert Meilaender, *Neither Beast Nor God: The Dignity of the Human Person* (New York: Encounter, 2009).

on the natural world with its oxygen, climate, and vegetation. We are also dependent on others with whom we are in a relationship: parents, family, and friends. These are God-given goods of our humanity. Without them, we either cease to thrive or cease to exist.

Health

At the same time, Messer adds, "Health is not to be equated with the whole of human well-being (as in the World Health Organization definition), and Christian talk of 'wholeness' should be treated with considerable caution."[15] In 1948, the World Health Organization (WHO) defined "health" as "a state of complete physical, mental and social well-being and not merely the absence of disease or infirmity."[16] The WHO definition of health is too idealistic for life in a fallen world. Although we may appreciate the fact that the definition does not focus only on illness or disease, it is unclear what would constitute a "complete" state of these various capacities. This would make health a kind of perfectionism. Does anyone attain such a high standard as complete physical, mental, and social well-being? If so, for how long? Do these often-transient qualities not change over time? We would not want to say that losing some of our strength, memory, or hair with age is necessarily a lack of health. It just is what it means to be human in this embodied existence.

By 1984, the WHO had revised its definition to affirm that health is "the extent to which an individual or group is able to realize aspirations and satisfy needs to change or cope with the

[15] Messer, *Flourishing*, 202.

[16] WHO constitution, quoted in "Health and Well-Being," World Health Organization, accessed October 14, 2024, https://www.who.int/data/gho/data/major-themes/health-and-well-being.

environment."[17] But this still seems too grandiose and perfectionistic. Instead of the WHO definition, Messer borrows from theologian Karl Barth, who defined health as "the strength for human life."[18] According to Messer, this way of thinking "recognizes the character of embodied human life as a divine gift that comes with a divine call, it offers an account of physical and mental integration that captures another important insight expressed in Christian talk of wholeness, and it allows a balanced understanding of health as the 'capability, vigor, and freedom' to live a human life."[19] Living a genuinely human life, especially in a fallen world, must be tempered by certain realities such as the present embodiment, finitude, dependence, and relationality, as well as decline, disease, and death.

So, although health is a penultimate good concerned with proximate human ends, our health points to the ultimate end, the realization of our full humanity, in the same way Jesus now realizes his full resurrected humanity. To confuse proximate ends for the ultimate end is to make an idol of our fallen humanity, a form of self-worship.

Understanding health in this way helps us to understand disease, suffering, and other evils and, therefore, to understand better what the role of medicine is. "Diseases," argues Messer, "are to be understood as a particular class of threats to creaturely flourishing: internal states or processes that tend to disrupt or threaten the fulfillment of the proximate ends of embodied creaturely human

---

[17] National Academies of Science, Engineering, and Medicine, *Achieving Whole Health: A New Approach for Veterans and the Nation: Consensus Study Report*, ed. Alex H. Krist, Jeannette South-Paul, and Marc Meisnere (Washington, DC: National Academies, 2023), 33, https://nap.nationalacademies.org/read/26854/chapter/4.

[18] Messer, *Flourishing*, 202.

[19] Messer, 202.

life."[20] Illness or disease are those states of being that interfere with or diminish the "strength for human life" in the realization that the strength for human life is more modest than the idealized perfection implied in the WHO definition of health. The Hebrew notion of wholeness or *shalom* can be enjoyed quite apart from the maximization of our human capacities. This wholeness is tempered by the realities of life in a fallen world in such a way that a person with diminished capacities may still experience wholeness or *shalom*.

Flourishing

Some threats to creaturely flourishing—or "strength for human life"—are temporary and may be relatively benign, like the common cold or certain allergies. They do hinder creaturely flourishing but, typically, not as much as other threats. We might say they are conditions usually either endured until they pass or treated by over-the-counter medications. Other threats, like cancer or injuries sustained in a motor vehicle accident, may be more acute, requiring treatment because they impair strength for human life. Yet our embodiment, limitations, dependency, and relationality per se are not pathologies to be treated but gifts to be appreciated. Medicine's role is not to rid us of those embodied goods.

"Our embodied creaturely life," says Messer, "is both gift and summons. It is the good gift of God the Creator, and with the gift comes the Creator's liberating command of 'respect for life.'"[21] This respect for life is accompanied by the will to be healthy, the will to seek the "doing and being" of a particularly human kind of flourishing. The will to be healthy is not merely individual, but also

[20] Messer, 184.

[21] Messer, 176.

social and political since there are many aspects of human health and flourishing that are tied to socio-economic and political realities. One need only think of matters of public health to understand this. Malnourishment, epidemics, and even eugenics might be examples of health-related phenomena that have social and political implications.

Christians understand that health is not an eternal but a temporal and limited possession. Thus, in Christian anthropology there is some ambivalence about death and disease. Although they often wreak havoc on human flourishing, they will one day be eradicated. Physical disease and death are enemies, but they are the last enemy to be defeated when all things are subjected to Christ (1 Cor 15:28). "In Christian terms, the defeat of death is accomplished neither by seeking it nor by evading it as long as possible, but by being ready to meet it, when it comes to us, 'in sure and certain hope of the Resurrection to eternal life, through our Lord Jesus Christ,' to use Cranmer's resonant phrase [in the Book of Common Prayer]."[22]

Messer spells out the practical implications of this way of thinking about health, flourishing, and disease:

> The divine command to "will to be healthy" (Barth) signals a clear, albeit qualified, theological affirmation of the work of medicine and health. Since genuine health and healing are always God's gift, a false opposition between medicine and the Christian healing ministry should be resisted. . . . Not everyone will be cured, and even those who are ill die sooner or later—not only because medical skill and knowledge are incomplete, but because embodied life in this world

---

[22] Messer, 196.

> is finite. The task of healing (including medicine) therefore includes the call to continue caring when cure is no longer possible. The life of Christian communities should offer resources that can support this work of care and transform the way suffering is understood and experienced.[23]

These final pillars are reminders that medicine is a gift and that being a physician is a holy calling. In fact, one ancient apocryphal text, Sirach 38:1–4, says, "Give doctors the honor they deserve, for the Lord gave them their work to do. Their skill came from the Most High, and kings reward them for it. Their knowledge gives them a position of importance, and powerful people hold them in high regard. The Lord created medicines from the earth, and a sensible person will not hesitate to use them" (GNT). At the same time, the inevitability of disease and death in the temporal realm are reminders not to worship either medicine or health.

In the meantime—between now and the death of death—we have the warrant to use medicine as one facet of care, in the realization of medicine's and medical technology's limitations. There are, however, no limitations placed on care. Although there may be times when it is appropriate to discontinue treatment, it is never appropriate to discontinue care. The physician's covenant is *always to care* even when it is not possible to cure.[24]

---

[23] Messer, 197, 199.

[24] See William F. May, *The Physician's Covenant: Images of the Healer in Medical Ethics*, 2nd ed. (Louisville, KY: Westminster John Knox, 2000), 82.

3

The Physician's Covenant

The physician's freedom with first names and body contact signals a parental understanding of the healer's role. The white lab coat points to the scientific origin of medical authority and hints at the technician, the body mechanic, at work. The title "doctor," from its root, implies teaching, while the term "professional," in root, suggests the notion of a covenant, a declaration or vow to be faithful to something for someone. Finally, the language of war dominates the modern understanding of disease and shapes the professional's response. The heart suffers an attack; cancers invade and spread like a conquering army; researchers look for a magic bullet.

—William F. May, *The Physician's Covenant*

Relationship between Physician and Patient

The relationship between a physician and his or her patient is central in medicine. This may seem obvious, but with the introduction of third-party payers (Medicare and insurance companies), corporate for-profit hospitals, and a litigious society, the relationship is either blurred, truncated, or sometimes turned on its head.

The provider of services model (PSM) of the physician-patient relationship is a contractual and consumerist model of medicine. It has become an all-too-common way of thinking about the roles of medicine, insurance companies, physicians, and patients. In the PSM, physicians and their health-care colleagues are merely "providers." In fact, we are often asked, "Who is your health-care provider?" Health-care providers have goods and services to offer, and they essentially make contracts with patients to pay for those goods and services. As consumer/customer, the patient is in the driver's seat, and as the saying goes, the customer is always right. If you do not believe it, just ask those patients who come to their doctor with a fistful of material they printed from the internet that includes what they think are their symptoms, what they believe is the recommended course of treatment, and nearly demanding that the physician provide what they request. Historically speaking, as physician paternalism has waned and patient autonomy has ascended, the PSM has become status quo in contemporary American medicine.

The traditional view, by contrast, is the Covenantal Perspective (CP) outlined in this chapter. One of the best articulations of the CP is by William F. May. May was for many years the Cary M. Maguire Professor of Ethics at Southern Methodist University. Not only was he one of the founders of the Hastings Center (the first bioethics think tank in America), from 2002 to 2004 he served on the US President's Council on Bioethics. He was one of those cadre of theologian-ethicists who helped shape the field of medical ethics in the late twentieth century. In his masterful volume, *The Physician's Covenant: Images of the Healer in Medical Ethics*, May compares and contrasts a contractual model with a covenantal model in medicine. Before examining his argument, it is important to be reminded of the nature of the biblical covenants and the covenantal tradition.

Ancient Near Eastern Covenants

In the ancient Near Eastern world—including the world of the Bible—covenants were a common way of defining the relationship between various parties. Broadly speaking, there were two types of covenantal relationships in the ancient world: suzerainty relationships and parity relationships. Suzerainty covenants governed the relationship between unequal parties, like a king with those who lived in his realm, sometimes called vassals. Parity covenants governed the relationship between equal parties, like one member of the realm with another member of the realm, vassal to vassal.[1]

A good example of a suzerainty covenant is the covenant God made with Abram (Genesis 17). God came to Abram when Abram was ninety-nine years old and revealed his authority to make the covenant: "I am God Almighty" (v. 1a). This was no covenant between equals. God is the sovereign king. He himself, as God,

[1] For a detailed description of ancient Near Eastern covenants, including the Old Testament covenant structure, see Meredith G. Kline, *Treaty of the Great King: The Covenant Structure of Deuteronomy* (Grand Rapids: Eerdmans, 1963); J. A. Thompson, *Ancient Near Eastern Treaties and the Old Testament* (Carol Stream, IL: Tyndale, 1963).

initiates the covenant with Abram. Notice also that the covenant is not conditional: "Live in my presence and be blameless. I will set up my covenant between me and you, and I will multiply you greatly" (vv. 1b–2). Here, the covenant is simply provided by God's good pleasure. He does not require anything from Abram, not even obedience as a condition. That is, God himself will set up and execute his covenant quite apart from any quid pro quo from Abram. He does not say, "I will multiply you greatly in return for this or that." In fact, all of the requirements for the execution of the covenant rested on God himself by his own sovereign will.

> "As for me, here is my covenant with you: You will become the father of many nations. Your name will no longer be Abram; your name will be Abraham, for I will make you the father of many nations. I will make you extremely fruitful and will make nations and kings come from you. I will confirm my covenant that is between me and you and your future offspring throughout their generations. It is a permanent covenant to be your God and the God of your offspring after you. And to you and your future offspring I will give the land where you are residing—all the land of Canaan—as a permanent possession, and I will be their God." (17:4–8)

There were certainly ways Abram and his descendants were meant to respond to the covenant. They were to obey the covenant, circumcise their male children, and follow the will of the Lord, but God never said that if they did not, he would revoke his covenant. In fact, the entire history of the people of God from that time until now is ample evidence that God has kept his covenant promise even though his people often failed to obey him. Paul makes much of the fact that their disobedience, and ours for that matter, could not invalidate the covenant ratified by the Almighty himself (Gal 3:15–29). This is a suzerainty covenant.

Alternatively, a parity covenant reflects a relationship between equal parties and typically has covenant stipulations that are conditional in nature. To put it in a more contemporary context, let us assume that you need a new roof on your house. You would work with your insurance company to locate an appropriate roofing contractor. You would establish a parity covenant, or contract. What would your relationship look like?

First, it is a relationship between equal parties. You are both tax-paying citizens, residents of a particular locale, and otherwise defined as equals before the law, regardless of rank, status, race, class, gender, and so on.

Second, you will enter a legal contract that specifies the goods and services that will define the relationship. This will include the supplies (shingles, nails, etc.) and labor costs. The contract will include stipulations about guarantees of the quality of those goods and services. Typically, the labor will be ensured for a year, sometimes more, and the materials for up to twenty years, depending on the roofing you choose. Should either of the parties renege on their contractual obligations, appeals for recourse would be made to the courts.

Third, your relationship with the contractor would be a self-interested, quid pro quo relationship. Your interest is in a new roof, and the contractor's interest is in a return on his labor, an income. He guarantees goods and services in exchange for payment. Because your insurance company is involved as a third party, the insurer will also have a stake in the outcome of the project and will want input about the type of materials, the means of attaching those materials, and the legal status of the contractor (whether he is ensured, has worker's compensation for his employees, and more).

Fourth, the contract will be of limited duration and application. It will apply only to the roof. The roofing contract, by definition, will not include repairs on an automobile or other things. It applies only to the roof and items directly associated with the roof replacement. Furthermore, the contract only covers the duration specified (e.g., one year on the labor and, say, twenty on the materials). Once the roof project is completed, and given that the materials and labor hold up, you and your contractor will have no enduring relationship. You have your roof; he has his paycheck. The deal is done.

This is a description of a typical contractual relationship. As May observes, "Contract and covenant, materially considered, appear to be first cousins; they both include an agreement and exchange between parties. But in spirit, contract and covenant differ markedly. Contractors are external; covenants are internal to the parties involved."[2] To understand what this means, and how the CP differs from the PSM, let us look more closely at the physician's covenant.

The Physician's Covenant

The physician's covenant is decidedly not between equal parties in a relevant way. A physician is a professional with knowledge of a vast science (biology, physiology, anatomy, chemistry, etc.), with specialty training (e.g., family medicine, surgery, reproductive endocrinology, psychiatry, anesthesia), holding an advanced degree with supervised training under one or more seasoned professionals, and held to high professional standards and virtues that extend beyond

---

[2] William F. May, *The Physician's Covenant: Images of the Healer in Medical Ethics*, 2nd ed. (Louisville, KY: Westminster John Knox, 2000), 127.

the stipulations of contract law. The science and the art of medicine are built on centuries of discovery, research, and experience. After all, human lives hang in the balance.

For a variety of reasons, the patient is not an equal party to the physician. First, the patient does not possess the knowledge, training, skills, experience, instruments, specialty knowledge, and formative practices of the physician. Second, the patient is vulnerable. Presumably she is suffering from either the effects of illness or the prospect of illness. Likely she came to the physician in a state of "dis-ease," hoping to learn the cause of the illness and anticipating some form of healing. She lacks the knowledge, tools, and formative practices to heal herself. That is why she is seeking the aid of a medical professional.

Another feature of the covenantal relationship between unequals is trust. The patient is trusting that the physician is working for his best interests and not for the minimalistic stipulations of a contract. He is trusting that his doctor is interested in his overall well-being—his flourishing—not merely that he pays the bill when the office visit or hospital procedure is complete. Because of that trust, physicians are permitted to do things (e.g., palpate, draw blood, make incisions in the body) that in any other context we would deem physical abuse or battery.

A contract is of limited duration, but the physician's covenant is an enduring or durable covenant, not circumscribed by the day or hour but by the patient's need. Because of the training and trust provided by society to physicians as professionals, in cases of extreme need—think of a motor vehicle accident or a person having a heart attack on an airplane—physicians cannot say, "I'm sorry. I'm off for the evening and cannot provide emergency care for you." Like the covenant God made with his people to protect them with a cloud by day and fire by night, as professionals, physicians are morally (and in some cases legally) obligated to provide care for those in dire need whether the doctor has finished the clinical day or not. It is a responsibility vested in the profession and, therefore, part of the physician's covenant. As May puts it, "Initiation into a profession means, in effect, that the physician is a healer when healing and when sleeping, when practicing and when malpracticing."[3] This points to another aspect of professionalism: a physician (or lawyer or minister) is a physician whether on the clock or off the clock, as it were.

Finally, the physician's covenant is donative. It is a gift relationship not grounded in a quid pro quo, including the ability of the patient to pay. The traditional professions—clergy, medicine, and law—each include the expectation that at least some of the work will be done pro bono. So again, in a dire situation, say, at a car wreck, physicians will not ask for proof of insurance or ability to pay before offering emergency care. Failure to treat under those circumstances would be a violation of the physician's covenantal obligations, professional virtues, and responsibilities assumed by society, not to mention being inhuman.

Of course, this does not mean that physicians cannot take time off or do not get a vacation. But it does mean that the covenantal relationship between physicians and patients is enduring and based on vulnerability, not on money. This obligation extends beyond physicians to those who have specialized training in patient care, such as nurses. As May argues:

> Contract medicine encourages not only minimalism, it also provokes a kind of maximalism, "defensive medicine." Under the pressure of the fear of disease and death, patients

---

[3] May, 127.

> often push for the maximum in tests and procedures, and physicians often yield to (or exploit) these fears, because they fear malpractice suits. Paradoxically, contractualism tempts the doctor simultaneously to do too little and too much for the patient—too little in that one extends oneself only to the limits the contract specifies, and too much in that one orders procedures that are useful in pampering the patients and protecting oneself, even though the patient's condition does not demand them.[4]

The Physician's Virtues

Although we have been exploring in many ways what physicians are obligated to do, it is also crucial to understand who physicians are meant to be. The virtues of the profession are to be embodied in the professional. In their twin volumes, *The Virtues in the Medical Practice* and *The Christian Virtues in Medical Practice*,[5] Edmund Pellegrino and David Thomasma offer an exposition of the virtues of "good doctors." Space does not provide a full accounting of that exposition, but understanding who doctors are meant to be is an essential aspect of understanding the role medicine is to play.

In the Aristotelian tradition, virtues are dispositions of character. The virtues are habits acquired by practice, repeated over and over again, just as athletic skills are acquired and refined by repeated practice. In a metaphorical way, just as athletic practice trains the

---

[4] May, 131.

[5] Edmund D. Pellegrino and David C. Thomasma, *The Virtues in Medical Practice* (Oxford: Oxford University Press, 1993); Edmund D. Pellegrino and David C. Thomasma, *The Christian Virtues in Medical Practice* (Washington, DC: Georgetown University Press, 1996).

body to act and react in certain ways through the development of muscle memory and eye-hand coordination, so the practice of virtuous behavior trains moral muscle memory to do the right thing without having to run ethical calculations for every decision. The virtues become part of the physician's way of inhabiting the world. The practice of medicine is a "habit of mind," heart, and will.

Fidelity to Trust

The first virtue Pellegrino and Thomasma explore should be apparent to us from the previous discussion; it is fidelity to trust: "Trust is ineradicable in human relationships. Without it we could not live in society or attain even the rudiments of a fulfilling life. Without trust we could not anticipate the future, and we would therefore be paralyzed into inaction. Yet to trust and entrust is to become vulnerable and dependent on the good will and motivations of those we trust."[6]

As professionals (and as human beings, for that matter), physicians should embody faithful responsibility to the trust that has been vested in them by their patients, their profession, and society. And what is it that patients expect from physicians? That they are working toward the patient's good, toward their well-being and flourishing. Though there is much in that notion of the patient's good, it is the basic requirement of moral medicine. Medicine is first, and foremost, for the patient's good.

Imagine that you are in a foreign country where you do not know the language. Imagine that you are in a motor vehicle accident. Now imagine that you are rushed to a large building, wheeled into a brightly lit room, surrounded by half a dozen

---

[6] Pellegrino and Thomasma, *Virtues in Medical Practice*, 65.

people dressed in pale blue uniforms. Each of them begins to do something to your body. One puts an oxygen mask over your nose and mouth. Another begins to inject some medication into your vein. Yet another attaches electrodes to your chest. Finally, someone in a long white coat comes to the side of your gurney and begins to examine you. As you focus your eyes on the people attending to you, what is your deepest hope? That they are there for your good and not to do harm. You are trusting that this is a hospital and that these are trained professionals, not members of a gang who are stealing the organs of tourists to sell on the black market. You are trusting that they will be faithful to the trust inherent in the relationship between a patient and those who care for him or her.

Virtue of Compassion

Furthermore, physicians should embody the virtue of compassion. "Compassion," maintain Pellegrino and Thomasma, "is an essential virtue of medical practice."[7] You are hoping that, even though you have never seen those who are working around your bedside before, they are compassionate individuals who, as the word "compassion" literally means, are coming alongside you as a fellow sufferer. They are co-sufferers. They know what it is like to be in pain, to be vulnerable, to be in need of the beneficent ministry of others. In important ways, they feel your pain and are loathe to contribute to more suffering. Whether this compassion is motivated by a Christian obligation to love one's neighbor as oneself or by simple common humanity does not matter at the moment. Compassion is not mere empathy, mercy, or pity. Compassion "includes an ability

[7] Pellegrino and Thomasma, 79.

to objectify what another person is feeling in symbolic form, that is, in our speech, our body language, and our participation in the 'story' of the other's illness."[8]

Unlike other friends who may feel compassion for a person experiencing illness, the physician brings something others typically lack—the technical and scientific knowledge and clinical experience that put the patient's story within the context of others with the same symptoms, disabilities, or disease. This is another reason good communication is so important. The virtue of compassion is not just about some generic or abstract patient. It is about this patient, with this experience of suffering, at this time.

Virtue of Phronesis

The third virtue of the good physician is what Pellegrino and Thomasma call "medicine's indispensable virtue"[9]—*phronesis.* Readers of Aristotle, Aquinas, and classical literature will know that phronesis is prudence or practical wisdom. Prudence is the reflex to recognize good and to apply it in particular acts. It is not speculative knowledge but a right way of acting. It does not imply certainty or infallibility, but rather that the application of wisdom is aimed at appropriate ends.

Of course, for the Christian, the right way of acting is consistent with the revealed will of God. That is why neighbor love and the Samaritan imperative have been prime motivators behind a Christian vision for the role of medicine. After all, Jesus himself taught that loving neighbor as oneself was a summary of our duties

[8] Pellegrino and Thomasma, 82.

[9] Pellegrino and Thomasma, 84.

to one another. Likewise, he taught that the human objects of love were not to be measured by their social worth but by their need as images of God who are suffering and vulnerable. This is one of the great lessons of the story of the Good Samaritan.

In *The Christian Virtues in Medical Practice*, Pellegrino and Thomasma point to a love-based (agapeistic) ethic that is by nature virtue-based.[10] Love is not a rule to be followed as much as it is a disposition to be inhabited in practices that reflect the virtue. Principles, rules, and duties are important to be sure, but the motivation to follow them is love. "Beneficence—acting for the good of the patient—is the central principle of medical ethics,"[11] they affirm. Because beneficence is motivated by love and not merely by, say, a financial responsibility, "medical knowledge is not proprietary or simply a means to a living. . . . Meeting the claims of the vulnerable is an essential feature of Christian belief. It is not optional or heroic. The healing ministry of the church is not an appendage through which compassion is titrated. It is the presence of Christ in the world."[12]

Virtuous Christian Health-Care Professionals

The virtues outlined previously continue to inform and motivate and are embodied in physicians and other health-care professionals today. During the COVID-19 crisis of 2019, the Christian Medical and Dental Associations (CMDA), an organization of

[10] Pellegrino and Thomasma, 73.
[11] Pellegrino and Thomasma, 74.
[12] Pellegrino and Thomasma, 75.

more than 13,000 Christian medical professionals, produced a policy statement titled "Duties of Christian Health Care Professionals in the Face of Pandemic Infection."[13] The CMDA based its statement on "a desire to share God's love and follow the example of Christ." They also rooted their case for care in the legacy of Christians in the past who served sacrificially in periods of epidemics, such as the great plagues. "Throughout the ages," they observe, "Christians—often at significant risk to themselves—have cared for victims of disasters and infectious diseases, leaving us a worthy legacy to emulate."[14] For Christian physicians, providing care in a time of pandemic is not a work of supererogation (going above and beyond the call of duty) but an expression of "ordinary" Christian love.

And as Charles Rosenberg shows in his volume, *The Care of Strangers: The Rise of the American Hospital System*, the modern hospital owes its origins to virtuous individuals who embodied Judeo-Christian love and compassion.[15] Evidence of this is the vast system of faith-based hospitals around the world with names like St. Vincent's, St. Luke's, Mt. Sinai, Presbyterian, Mercy, Beth Israel, Methodist, and Baptist. The Red Cross and the hospice movement are other examples of Christian virtue in action.

---

[13] This statement, along with many other ethics and policy statements, may be found at "Position & Public Policy Statements," CMDA website, accessed October 14, 2024, https://cmda.org/policy-issues-home/position-statements/.

[14] CMDA, "Duties of Christian Health Care Professionals in the Face of Pandemic Infection," 1. See CMDA, "Position & Public Policy Statements."

[15] Charles E. Rosenberg, *The Care of Strangers: The Rise of the American Hospital System* (New York: Basic Books, 1987).

The Choreography of Care

One important reason for reflecting on these models is because, from the days of Hippocrates until around the middle of the twentieth century, physician paternalism characterized the relationship between a doctor and his (a physician was almost always a male) patient. After all, Hippocrates is credited with saying, "Life is short, and the Art long; the occasion fleeting; experience fallacious, and judgement difficult. The physician must not only be prepared to do what is right himself, but also to make the patient, the attendants, and externals co-operate."[16] This can certainly be taken to entail strong paternalism. Note the verb "making." The physician makes the patient and everyone else cooperate. This is quite a prescription. Doctor knows best! With this kind of strong paternalism, the relationship between a physician and her patient can easily become adversarial. In fact, the history of medical jurisprudence is punctuated by wars among physicians, patients, families, and third-party payers.

Today, however, for some relatively good reasons and for some less good reasons, physician paternalism has given way to its polar opposite, patient autonomy. Danial Callahan was a philosopher and the co-founder of the world's first bioethics think tank, the Hastings Center. In a penetrating essay about legalized euthanasia in the center's journal, Callahan rightly chastens this reversal. He concludes that "the problem is precisely that, too often in human history, killing has seemed the quick, efficient way to put aside that which burdens us. It rarely helps, and too often simply adds to one evil still another. That is what I believe euthanasia would

---

[16] Oath of Hippocrates, in *Harvard Classics*, vol. 38 (Boston: P. F. Collier and Son, 1910).

accomplish. It is self-determination run amok."[17] Although it is demonstrable historically that medicine has sometimes—or more properly, physicians have sometimes—been guilty of strong paternalism, adopting absolute patient autonomy seems too radical for the well-being of patients and the types of treatment they sometimes desperately require.

Granted, there are extremes to be avoided; and granted, the patient's body is the patient's property, as it were. But medicine deserving of the name cannot be governed by naked self-determination. After all, as we have seen, the word "patient" comes from a root that means "sufferer." The sufferer is compromised by "dis-ease" that he or she presumably cannot remedy. So, the patient appeals to the physician, who is pledged to work for the good of the patient.

I have described the physician-patient relationship as being more like dance than a DIY project. In a dance the partners both have an important role to play. One leads and the other follows, but neither works independently of the other; neither partner is autonomous, and there are rules and patterns to follow.

I was encouraged to find a seasoned physician-ethicist using the same metaphor. "When we remember that medicine is a human activity like dancing," Abraham J. Nussbaum says, "we can account for the mutual responsibility of both dancers."[18] Nussbaum attributes this metaphor to social theorist Charles Taylor. "Taylor," he points out, "offered dancing as a paradigmatic social practice because it involves constant interplay between people, a give-and-take. We

---

[17] Udo Schuklenk and Peter Singer, eds., *Bioethics: An Anthology*, 4th ed. (Hoboken, NJ: Wiley, 2022), 355.

[18] Abraham M. Nussbaum, *The Finest Traditions of My Calling: One Physician's Search for the Renewal of Medicine* (New Haven, CT: Yale University Press, 2016), 111.

could likewise see offering and receiving medical care as a social practice akin to dancing."[19] In Taylor's own words, "A very important feature of human action is rhythming, cadence. Every apt, coordinated gesture has a certain flow. When you lose this, as occasionally happens, you fall into confusion, your actions become inept and uncoordinated."[20] This last line, unfortunately, characterizes too much of modern medicine and too many of the relationships between doctors and their patients. As well-intentioned and necessary as they might be, third-party payers—and other parties—only complicate the dance.

> We could also remember that just as a dancer may lead at one moment and be led at another, our roles as patients and physicians are fluid: all of us who are physicians at present will some day be patients ourselves and will have to learn those unfamiliar steps. Remembering the way our roles change over time—from patient to physician to patient—is part of understanding medicine as a social practice with common rhythms. We learn medicine through participation in relationships that are like dances—formed by apprenticing to expert physicians and listening to patients—with rules learned through social practices.[21]

Contemporary patient care is in desperate need of an ethic that avoids the extremes of both paternalism and autonomy. The

[19] Nussbaum, 109.

[20] Charles Taylor, *Philosophical Arguments* (Cambridge, MA: Harvard University Press, 1995), 172. Cited in Nussbaum, *Finest Traditions of My Calling*, 109.

[21] Nussbaum, *Finest Traditions of My Calling*, 111.

patient is a person and so is the physician. The healing dance—or the treatment tango, if you will—requires partners who are willing to respect one another, negotiate their relationship, and take steps together that move the patient toward well-being and optimal flourishing of the sort we saw in the previous chapter.

4

Ethics at the Edges of Life

I venture to believe there may be a truly *humanistic* ethics which acknowledges the awesome claims and entitlements of another human life simply because he or she is a human being. Where I would be inclined to say the "sanctity" of human life, the reader may choose rather to say the "dignity" of human life. There may be a vector of convergence between religious ethics and humanistic ethics, so long as the value of *human* life is not allowed to acquire a generic meaning—species life, familial life, social life—which obliterates the individual who (the religious say) is still our neighbor whatever may be his or her condition or achievement or duration or productivity.

—Paul Ramsey, *Ethics at the Edges of Life: Medical and Legal Intersections*

Many of the questions about ethics at the edges of life—at its beginning and its end—arise because of contemporary technology, but perhaps not the most obvious one. The technology that most impacted medicine in the modern era was not the PCR (polymerase chain reaction) machine that made genetic analysis possible. It was not the mechanical ventilator that made it possible to help a comatose patient breathe. It was not even the dialysis machine that purifies waste products from kidneys or the pig valve for treating human heart disease. The technology that most altered modern medicine was flexible plastic tubing. Without flexible plastic tubing, none of those other technologies would be possible. The invention of flexible plastic tubing is not the cause per se, but it provided a new means of treatment that now raises important benefits and, sometimes, burdens.

Although technology clearly has a role to play, the central feature of ethics at the edges of life is the nature of the human person, the limits of technology, and who decides who lives or dies. Let us begin at the beginning.

The Nuptial Covenant and the Ethics of Human Procreation

In the beginning, human beings were created according to God's good design. They are made in his own image, the *imago Dei*. Imagers of God are given the commission to be stewards of his creation and to procreate (see Gen 1:26–29; 9:1–6). As sovereign Creator, God could have made humans single-sex organisms—self-propagating parthenogens like aphids, Indo-Pacific geckos, or the velvet worm. Instead, in Genesis 2—the divinely inspired commentary on Genesis 1—we are told that God's purpose in creating male and female is so that the "man leaves his father and his mother and bonds with his wife, and they become one flesh" (Gen 2:24). This one-flesh union is the biblical nuptial covenant—from the Latin *nuptialis* "pertaining to marriage," from *nuptiae* "a wedding"—the covenant of marriage.

One fully embodied male made in God's image would engage in covenantal, procreative union with one fully embodied female made in God's image; and from their union, offspring—male and female—would continue to follow the mandate to be fruitful, multiply, and fill the earth, with image and likeness passed from one generation to the next (Gen 5:1–3). It is within this covenantal, procreative union that God has been pleased to bless the gift of children, and he calls on parents to safeguard and steward this gift for his glory, the benefit of his church, and the good of the entire race. Thus, procreation is as much a part of the dominion or stewardship mandate as tending the garden. In that mandate, there is a presumption in favor of procreation.

This was the view of the early church, Roman Catholicism, and the Protestant Reformers. It needs no defense here. In fact, their repudiations of the violations of the nuptial covenant, including repudiation of birth control and abortion, is breathtaking by today's standards. For example, in the *Didache* (AD 50–70) or The Teaching of the Twelve Apostles (an early handbook to guide new Christians), we find it stated straightforwardly: "Do not kill a fetus by abortion, or commit infanticide."[1] Other examples from the history of the early church could be multiplied. Suffice it to say that beyond merely a consensus opposing abortion, infanticide, and birth control, early Christians celebrated childbirth and were instrumental in welcoming children and caring for infants, whether

[1] Harry J. Gensler, *Ethics: A Contemporary Introduction* (New York: Routledge, 1998), 181.

their own or those abandoned by others. They built orphanages and foundling hospitals as ways of celebrating the sanctity of every human life and protecting children.

By the time of the European Enlightenment, untethered from the teaching of Scripture, Western culture came to focus on the autonomous individual, the "I am" of Descartes's *cogito ergo sum*. This evolution has been well traced by Alasdair MacIntyre, Charles Taylor, Michael Sandel, and most recently, Carl Trueman. What Sandel calls the "unencumbered self"[2] is defined by the self's capacity to choose. It is essentially the expression of the human will with a body in tow. This sovereign self is king in contemporary culture.

With the sexual revolution of the 1960s, this self was increasingly exalted, sexualized, and politicized in the culture wars over contraception, abortion, reproductive technologies, and now, gender identity. Today, the human person has become a naked "self"—a do-it-yourself project—created in one's own preferred image.

Like nearly everyone else in the Western cultural soup, evangelical Protestants also came to see themselves mostly as lone, unencumbered, autonomous, expressive individuals. They abandoned the implications of the nuptial covenant: first, by seeing marriage as yet another self-improvement project; second, by conceding to contraception; and finally, by being lured into some of the more subtle habits of the sexual revolution, including our current practice of treating a perfectly healthy body as a pathology that requires hormonal or surgical mutilations to keep it from functioning normally, as with transgender modifications, but we have been doing it for decades with hormonal contraception and sterilization.

---

[2] Michael J. Sandel, *Democracy's Discontent: A New Edition for Our Perilous Times* (Cambridge, MA: Harvard University Press, 2022), 111.

The Birth Control Revolution

Although barrier methods of birth control (e.g., condoms) have been around for thousands of years, contraceptive technologies like the IUD (intrauterine device) and the contraceptive pill are twentieth-century inventions. As social historian Allan Carlson has shown in *Godly Seed*, his brilliant yet heartbreaking history of American evangelicals and birth control from 1873–1973, American evangelical Protestants were the ones "who [had at one time] waged the most aggressive and effective campaigns against the practice of birth control within the United States." It was evangelicals "who—starting in 1873—successfully built a web of federal and state laws that equated contraception with abortion, suppressed the spread of birth control information and devices, and even criminalized the use of contraceptives."[3]

But the tides changed in the early part of the twentieth century. Lockstep with the ascension of the sovereign self, artificial birth control was introduced into the evangelical Christian imagination. In 1930, among British Anglicans for instance, the Lambeth Conference offered a dozen resolutions on marriage under the more general rubric of "The Life and Witness of the Christian Community." By presumably unanimous consent, Resolution 9 states, "The Conference believes that the conditions of modern life call for a fresh statement from the Christian Church on the subject of sex. It declares that the functions of sex as a God-given factor in human life are essentially noble and creative. Responsibility in regard to their right use needs the greater emphasis in view of widespread laxity of thought and conduct in all these matters."

---

[3] Allan Carlson, *Godly Seed: American Evangelicals Confront Birth Control, 1873–1973* (New York: Routledge, 2011), 1.

Resolution 10 confesses, "The Conference believes that in the exalted view of marriage taught by our Lord is to be found the solution of the problems with which we are faced. His teaching is reinforced by certain elements which have found a new emphasis in modern life, particularly the sacredness of personality, the more equal partnership of men and women, and the biological importance of monogamy."[4]

In Resolution 14 we read, "The Conference affirms: the duty of parenthood as the glory of married life; the benefit of a family as a joy in itself, as a vital contribution to the nation's welfare, and as a means of character-building for both parents and children; the privilege of discipline and sacrifice to this end." So far, perhaps, so good.

But in Resolution 15 a tectonic shift occurs. By a vote of 193 to 67 (with 46 abstaining), the bishops opined:

> Where there is a clearly felt moral obligation to limit or avoid parenthood, the method must be decided on Christian principles. The primary and obvious method is complete abstinence from intercourse (as far as may be necessary) in a life of discipline and self-control lived in the power of the Holy Spirit. Nevertheless, in those cases where there is such a clearly felt moral obligation to limit or avoid parenthood, and where there is a morally sound reason for avoiding complete abstinence, the Conference agrees that other methods may be used, provided that this is done in the light of the same Christian principles. The Conference records its strong condemnation of the use of

---

[4] Note that phrase "particularly the sacredness of personality." I have been unable to find a commentary on the meaning and weight of that phrase in its context.

> any methods of conception control from motives of selfishness, luxury, or mere convenience.[5]

As Carlson puts it, "So ended the 1,800-year-old Christian consensus on birth control."[6]

There was, to be sure, some unhappiness in traditional quarters, especially from the leading Anglo-Catholic theologian of the day, Bishop Charles Gore, who declared, "The Church has regarded Birth Prevention as sinful because, like other sensual practices commonly called unnatural, it is a deliberate enterprise taken in hand to separate absolutely the enjoyment of the sexual act from its natural issue. It is thus to be reckoned among the unfruitful works of darkness."[7]

What were the sources of this "clearly felt moral obligation" in the Lambeth opinion? Why 1930? Certain ideas were swirling in the cultural vortex at the turn of the century. Malthusian fears of overpopulation were rising, and social Darwinism was doing its corrosive work in the culture so that, by 1930, the British and American eugenics movements were at their apogee. In England, Darwin's cousin, Francis Galton, created a Eugenics Record Office in 1904. Following downstream in the United States, Charles Davenport founded the Eugenics Record Office in Cold Springs Harbor, New York, in 1910. American eugenicists

---

[5] Anglican Communion Office et al., "Resolution 15—The Life and Witness of the Christian Community–Marriage," Anglican Communion website, accessed October 14, 2024, https://www.anglicancommunion.org/resources/document-library/lambeth-conference/1930/resolution-15-the-life-and-witness-of-the-christian-community-marriage.aspx.

[6] Carlson, *Godly Seed*, 103.

[7] See Peter Sedgwick, "The Lambeth Conferences on Contraception, 1908–1968," *Theology* 123, no. 2 (2022): 95–103, https://www.researchgate.net/publication/339794961_The_Lambeth_Conferences_on_contraception_1908-68.

included well-known titans such as George Bernard Shaw, Oliver Wendell Holmes, John Harvey Kellogg, J. P. Morgan, and Andrew Carnegie. The churches were also complicit. The Protestant Social Gospel preachers, aided and abetted by a naïve postmillennialism, were heralding the promises of eugenics to create a better educated and "fitter" society. There were sermon contests for the best homilies supporting eugenics. In the United States, awards were given to the "Fitter Family" at eugenics fairs across the nation.[8]

On the other side, the razor-sharp Christian apologist G. K. Chesterton decried the burgeoning eugenics movement in his 1922 publication, *Eugenics and Other Evils*. It was Chesterton, with his characteristic turn of a phrase, who called the "new morality a filthy thing which avoids birth and abandons control."[9] Just a few months after the 1930 Lambeth Conference, the Roman Catholic Church published its encyclical, *Casti Connubii*, reaffirming the church's views on the sanctity of marriage and the purpose of sexuality. At the same time, the Roman Catholic Church expressed profound opposition to eugenics, birth control, and abortion.

It will come as no surprise to those who know history that Margaret Sanger, the founder of Planned Parenthood in 1916, was a racist, radical eugenicist, and pro-abortionist. Sanger celebrated the Lambeth statement, exclaiming that it "was inevitably to lead the way toward the crystallization of a universal Protestant acceptance of the moral necessity of birth control."[10] It was Sanger and Planned Parenthood who aided Gregory Pincus and John Rock in

---

[8] See "Fitter Family Contests," Eugenics Archive, accessed October 14, 2024, https://www.eugenicsarchive.ca/connections?id=535eebfb7095aa0000000228.

[9] G. K. Chesterton, *Eugenics and Other Evils* (London: Cassell, 1922); https://www.gutenberg.org/files/25308/25308-h/25308-h.htm.

[10] Carlson, *Godly Seed*, 104.

the development of the first birth control pill in the late 1950s. Sanger and company led the campaign not only for artificial means of contraception but also for elective abortion as a means of birth control: essentially, procreative control by whatever means necessary. Population control, quality control, birth control. Control.

The 1958 Lambeth Conference went on record for "its profound conviction that the idea of the human family is rooted in the Godhead and that consequently all problems of sex relations, the procreation of children, and the organisation of family life must be related, consciously and directly, to the creative, redemptive, and sanctifying power of God" (Resolution 112). Furthermore, the conference called "responsible parenthood" a "right and important factor in Christian family life" that "should be the result of positive choice before God" (Resolution 115), adding that "the means of family planning are in large measure matters of clinical and ascetic choice . . . Christians have every right to use the gifts of science for proper ends."[11]

Contraception became just another expression of the will of the sovereign self. The church became complicit with the new forms of birth control and even chastised parents "who carelessly and improvidently bring children into the world, trusting in an unknown future or a generous society to care for them."[12] A short decade later, in 1968, the Lambeth bishops repudiated *Humanae Vitae's* pro-natal views on contraception. "Reproductive choice" with

---

[11] See Resolutions 112 and 115 on the website of the Anglican Communion, "Index of Resolutions from 1958," https://www.anglicancommunion.org/resources/document-library/lambeth-conference/1958/lambeth-conference-archives-1958-index?year=1958; The Anglican Communion, *The Encyclical Letter from the Bishops, Together with the Resolutions and Reports* (n.p.: SPCK, 1958), at 2.148, 2.147.

[12] Hubert Cunliffe-Jones, *A History of Christian Doctrine* (New York: T&T Clark, 2006), 562.

its freedom from the consequences of promiscuous sex made it possible to divorce children and family from the telos of sex and opened the door eventually to boundless freedom of sexual expression.

I wish we could say that the evangelical church merely got carried along in the torrent, but I think it largely swam with the flow. Evangelicals and other Christians have been complicit in the formation of a contraceptive culture. As Baylor University moral theologian Matthew Anderson says, "Now that we are almost a century out from Lambeth, though, every Protestant denomination has made its peace with contraception—either explicitly, or through a quiescent willingness to regard it as a matter for Christian debate."[13] Today, according to the Guttmacher Institute, the polling arm of Planned Parenthood, "Almost all women who identify as religious have ever used contraceptive methods—99 percent of mainline Protestants, evangelical Protestants and Catholics, and 96 percent of people with other religious affiliations."[14]

A thorough treatment of the consequences of contraceptive culture can be found in social commentator Mary Eberstadt's work. Premarital sex, abortion on demand, cohabitation, no-fault divorce, and single parenthood are downstream effects of a contraceptive culture. For example, a 2019 Pew Research survey found that 58 percent of white evangelicals and 70 percent of black Protestants believe cohabiting is acceptable if the couple plans to marry.[15]

---

[13] Alistair Roberts et al. *Protestant Social Teaching: An Introduction* (Landrum, SC: Davenant, 2022), 91.

[14] Rachel K. Jones, "People of All Religions Use Birth Control and Have Abortions," Guttmacher, October 2020, https://www.guttmacher.org/article/2020/10/people-all-religions-use-birth-control-and-have-abortions.

[15] David Ayers, "The Cohabitation Dilemma Comes for America's Pastors, *Christianity Today* (March 16, 2021). Also available at https://

What has all of this to do with medicine? Plenty. The evolution of the contraceptive culture would not have been possible without both the complicity of medicine and the emergence of the sovereign self, also known as patient autonomy. The combination of these two forces turned pregnancy into a condition to be addressed by medicine. But what does contraception have to do with health? Except in cases where a woman's menstrual cycle is irregular, a prescription for contraception does not contribute to a woman's health. On the contrary, although relatively safe, contraceptives may sometimes compromise a woman's health. And some forms of contraception (the IUD and others) may permit fertilization but prevent implantation of the embryo. These are abortifacient forms of contraception and cause lethal harm to the embryo, even if they do not cause direct harm to the mother.

Abortion

I was a high school student in the early 1970s when the abortion debate was reaching its apex, resulting in the 1973 Supreme Court decision *Roe v. Wade* and its companion ruling in *Doe v. Bolton*. At that time, the debate about the morality of abortion was framed by the question, "When does human life begin?" If one is honest, that question is no longer up for debate. Everyone knows that when a human egg and human sperm unite, at least one genetically unique human being comes into existence. Twinning is still possible at that stage, so it could be more than one, but at least one member of the species *Homo sapiens* emerges in the world. Any unbiased scientific

www.christianitytoday.com/2021/03/cohabitation-dilemma-comes-for-american-pastors-ayers/.

account will confirm this. For instance, one well-respected embryology textbook, now in its tenth edition, says:

> Human development begins at fertilization when a sperm fuses with an oocyte to form a single cell, the **zygote**. This highly specialized, *totipotent cell* (capable of giving rise to any cell type) marks the beginning of each of us as a unique individual. The zygote, just visible to the unaided human eye, contains chromosomes and genes that are derived from mother and father. The zygote divides many times and become progressively transformed into a multicellular human being through cell division, migration, growth, and differentiation.[16]

If a textbook definition is less than scintillating, perhaps the real-life story of a physician friend of mine will communicate better. As a twenty-eight-year-old OB/GYN resident physician, Steve Hammond began performing abortions to earn extra income during medical school. Under United States Supreme Court rulings handed down in *Roe v. Wade* (1973) and *Doe v. Bolton* (1973), abortion was legal for nearly any reason as long as a patient wanted one and a physician was willing to perform the procedure. Since abortions were legal, his patients wanted them, and he was good at doing them, Hammond performed more than 700 abortions.

---

[16] Keith L. Moore, T. V. N. Persaud, and Mark G. Torchia, *The Developing Human: Clinically Oriented Embryology*, 10th ed. (New York: Elsevier, 2020), 11; bold in original. For a scientific and philosophical account, see Robert P. George and Christopher Tollefsen, *Embryo: A Defense of Human Life* (New York: Doubleday, 2008); Samuel B. Condic and Maureen L. Condic, *Human Beings: A Scientific and Philosophical Approach* (Washington, DC: Catholic University of America Press, 2018).

It was "just another procedure," as he put it in his volume *The Christian and Abortion.*[17]

But one day, things changed. While he was performing an abortion, the baby kicked him. Not only that, when he put his hand on the woman's abdomen, he could feel the baby "squirming violently" inside her uterus. Only then did he discover that the patient had lied about how long she had been pregnant. She was not in her first trimester but was at least twenty-two weeks pregnant, maybe more.[18]

Although Hammond saw himself as a Christian, he had not put the puzzle together until that moment. He came to see himself as both morally and professionally responsible for taking human lives. Rather than blame his church for not teaching him better or his medical school for indoctrinating him during his education, he knew he was guilty of violating a cardinal rule of medical ethics: "Do no harm."

I came to know Steve many years later. Over lunch one day I asked, "If it had been illegal, would you still have performed abortions?" He replied without hesitation, "no, I would not have broken the law." He now understands that one of the reasons societies pass laws forbidding murder, prohibiting prostitution, and driving under the influence, is because those acts injure human lives and do not promote human flourishing. But under promiscuous legislation like *Roe* and *Doe*, abortion became an exception. For Steve, that all changed when another living human being kicked back while he was acting legally, but functioning immorally.

---

[17] Steve Hammond and Emily LaBonte, *The Christian and Abortion: A Nonnegotiable Stance* (Grand Rapids: Credo House, 2019), 23.

[18] Hammond and LaBonte, 23.

Laws may not be able to change attitudes, but they can encourage certain practices and penalize infractions of the law for the sake of preventing harm to oneself or others. Because the aim of medicine is human flourishing and because the unborn are humans, the role of medicine must include the flourishing of the unborn as well as the born. After all, the unborn and the already born are only separated by geography (i.e., either inside the womb or outside the womb). This reality has implications for artificial reproductive technologies like in vitro fertilization and others.

Artificial Reproductive Technologies

Louise Joy Brown was born July 25, 1978, and was heralded as the world's first "test tube baby." The reference to a test tube is shorthand for the fact that she was conceived through what was then a new reproductive technology, the method known as in vitro fertilization (IVF). *In vitro* means "in glass."

IVF is relatively simple. A woman is given drugs to stimulate ovulation. About a dozen ova are removed and placed in a petri dish (in vitro). Sperm are retrieved from a man and introduced into a medium with the ova. With little assistance, sperm and egg do what they naturally do. Sperm penetrates the egg, and hopefully, fertilization occurs. A fertilized egg is a zygote or early embryo, the terms used to describe the developmental stage of a very young human being. Again, this is unquestionably a living human being because it is only living human beings one wants to be transferred to a woman's uterus.

If, let us say, a dozen embryos are generated in vitro, only one to three of those embryos will be transferred to a woman's uterus. According to the recommendations of the American Society of

Reproductive Medicine (ASRM), the number depends somewhat on the gestational mother's age.[19] But for the safety of both the mother and the embryos, no more than three would be transferred to a woman's uterus. Statistically speaking, a relative few will survive and become what are known as "take home babies."

According to the Society for Assisted Reproductive Technology (SART), depending on the mother's age, 34 percent to 47 percent of IVF attempts result in live births.[20] What about the embryos who do not survive? "Embryo loss" is a euphemism for the death of an unborn human being. So between 53 percent and 66 percent die.[21] If there are ten embryos remaining after the first round of IVF, what happens to the others? There are only a few alternatives. The so-called spare embryos may be used in a future attempt to achieve a live birth (again, with the high likelihood some of the embryos will not survive). Embryos may also be offered for embryo adoption to another potential family. Remaining embryos have been used in research that results in the death of the embryo. Finally, the embryos can remain frozen for an indefinite period of time. Cryopreservation is not free, and we do not know how long frozen embryos can be preserved healthy. Eventually, they will die.

---

[19] The Practice Committee of the American Society for Reproductive Medicine and the Practice Committee of the Society for Assisted Reproductive Technology, "Guidelines on Number of Embryos Transferred" at https://www.fertstert.org/article/S0015-0282(09)03625-5/pdf.

[20] SART, "All SART Member Clinics: Final National Summary Report for 2021," sartcorsonline.com, accessed October 14, 2024, https://sartcorsonline.com/CSR/PublicSnapshotReport?ClinicPKID=0&reportingYear=2021.

[21] SART, "All SART Member Clinics."

Because, as has been argued, the provider of services model of medicine (PSM) is consumeristic, the ethics of artificial reproductive technology are largely determined by the marketplace. Sadly, IVF and other related procedures treat reproduction as a project and unborn human beings as a commodity or a product.[22]

At the Other End of Life

How one approaches ethics at the beginning of life will have profound implications for how one approaches ethics at the end of life because the threads connecting the two are (1) the nature of the human person as someone made in the image of God and (2) the role of the profession of medicine.

The movement to legalize physician-assisted suicide (PAS) in the United States continues to grow. The practice is currently legal in Oregon (1994), Washington (2008), Montana (2009), Vermont (2013), California (2016), Colorado (2016), Hawaii (2019), New Jersey (2019), Maine, (2019), and New Mexico (2021). PAS occurs when a physician provides a patient with medications that are intended to end the patient's life. The physician does not directly administer the drug but makes it available to the patient. Euthanasia refers to the practice of a physician actively administering a life-ending drug. Although currently illegal in the United States, along with assisted suicide, euthanasia has been legal in the Netherlands, Belgium, and Luxembourg since the 2000s. Colombia and Canada legalized euthanasia in 2015.

---

[22] For a very helpful theological treatment of IVF and other reproductive technologies, see Oliver O'Donovan, *Begotten or Made?* (Landrum, SC: Davenant, 2022).

Proponents of both PAS and euthanasia justify the practices on the basis of patient autonomy. Since it is the patient's life, he or she may end it when the patient deems life no longer worthy of living. Most PAS laws offer a set of conditions and a window of time. For instance, the Oregon law states: "An adult who is capable and has been determined by the attending physician and consulting physician to be suffering from a terminal disease, and who has voluntarily expressed his or her wish to die, may make a written request for medication for the purpose of ending his or her life in a humane and dignified manner."[23] Like the laws of other states, Oregon's law defines a terminal disease as "an incurable and irreversible disease that has been medically confirmed and will, within reasonable medical judgment, produce death within six months."[24] There are other stipulations, but these are the foundations of the law.

As we have seen in earlier chapters, both the ancient Hippocratic Oath and the Christian Hippocratic Oath prohibit a physician from either killing or being complicit in the killing of a patient. Doing so is contrary to the physician's professional covenantal obligations. Its justification, today, is a so-called right to die.

Technically speaking, rights and obligations are different sides of the same coin. To say that I have a right is to imply that others have an obligation either to provide the means for me to exercise that right or not to interfere in my exercise of that right. To say that I have a right to life, for instance, means that others have an obligation to assist me in living and not to hinder me from living.

---

[23] Oregon Health Authority, "Oregon Revised Statute: Oregon's Death with Dignity Act: Chapter 127," Oregon.gov, accessed October 14, 2024, https://www.oregon.gov/oha/ph/providerpartnerresources/evaluationresearch/deathwithdignityact/pages/ors.aspx.

[24] Oregon Health Authority, "Oregon Revised Statute."

Right-to-life legislation at the beginning of life means that the government recognizes the right of unborn human beings to be allowed to be born and that the government should do what it can to prevent unborn human beings from being killed.

How should we understand a right to die? What kind of liberty claim is it? If one has a right to die, what obligations are entailed by others? Although a right to die might mean no one should interfere in someone's death, how can my right to die obligate someone else to kill me or provide the means of my killing myself? This is a curious way of thinking about rights. There is something strange about using one's freedom to make a decision to end one's opportunity to make free decisions. But that is how the justification of right to die works. PAS requires not only a recognition of a patient's right to die but also the obligation of a physician to assist the patient in dying. Yet a physician never has an obligation to kill or assist in killing. Professionally speaking, the physician's role is to cure, and where curing is not possible, to care.

Some physicians are pushing back against the PAS-euthanasia juggernaut. The Christian Medical and Dental Associations (CMDA) and Physicians for Compassionate Care Educational Foundation (PCCEF), for instance, are on record as opposing PAS-euthanasia. Interestingly, even though PAS is increasingly becoming legal in the United States, the nation's largest physician organization continues to be opposed to it. It is worth noting the opinion of the American Medical Association (AMA) found in its Code of Medical Ethics:

> Physician-assisted suicide occurs when a physician facilitates a patient's death by providing the necessary means and/or information to enable the patient to perform the life-ending act (e.g., the physician provides sleeping pills

> and information about the lethal dose, while aware that the patient may commit suicide).
>
> It is understandable, though tragic, that some patients in extreme duress—such as those suffering from a terminal, painful, debilitating illness—may come to decide that death is preferable to life. However, permitting physicians to engage in assisted suicide would ultimately cause more harm than good.
>
> Physician-assisted suicide is fundamentally incompatible with the physician's role as healer, would be difficult or impossible to control, and would pose serious societal risks.
>
> Instead of engaging in assisted suicide, physicians must aggressively respond to the needs of patients at the end of life. Physicians:
>
> (a) Should not abandon a patient once it is determined that cure is impossible.
> (b) Must respect patient autonomy.
> (c) Must provide good communication and emotional support.
> (d) Must provide appropriate comfort care and adequate pain control.[25]

The CMDA's statement is even more explicit:

> We, as Christian physicians and dentists, believe that human life is a gift from God and is sacred because it bears

[25] AMA Code of Medical Ethics, "Opinion 5.7: Physician-Assisted Suicide," accessed October 14, 2024, https://code-medical-ethics.ama-assn.org/index.php/ethics-opinions/physician-assisted-suicide.

> God's image. Human life has worth because Christ died to redeem it, and it has meaning because God has an eternal purpose for it.
>
> We oppose active intervention with the intent to produce death for the relief of pain, suffering, or economic considerations, or for the convenience of patient, family, or society.
>
> Proponents of physician-assisted suicide argue from the perspective of compassion and radical individual autonomy. There are persuasive counter arguments based on the traditional norms of the medical professions and the adverse consequences of such a public policy. Even more important than these secular arguments is the biblical view that the sovereignty of God places a limit on human autonomy.
>
> In order to affirm the dignity of human life, we advocate the development and use of alternatives to relieve pain and suffering, provide human companionship, and give opportunity for spiritual support and counseling.
>
> The Christian Medical & Dental Associations oppose physician-assisted suicide in any form.[26]

Both the AMA and the CMDA recognize that physician-assisted suicide fundamentally changes the nature of the healing profession and the relationship between physicians and patients. When healers become killers, the consequences are grave (no pun intended).

---

[26] Collected and adapted from the individual statements at "Position & Public Policy Statements," CMDA website, accessed October 14, 2024, https://cmda.org/policy-issues-home/position-statements/.

The Better Way of Medicine

Instead of PAS and euthanasia, what is the better way? Is it ever permissible to say that the technology of medicine has done all it can do, and it is time to change the course of treatment? The answer is yes. There is a time to live and a time to die (Ecclesiastes 3). Even the best, most sophisticated medicine cannot prolong life indefinitely. Nor should it. There may come a time when it is appropriate to discontinue medical interventions.

But discontinuing treatment is not the same as discontinuing "care." There is never an appropriate reason to discontinue care. Bill Davis's extraordinarily helpful guide, *Departing in Peace: Biblical Decision-Making at the End of Life*, should be read by every Christian to help prepare them for making those decisions for themselves or for their loved ones. "Christians," Davis reminds us, "should be among the first to acknowledge that medical efforts cannot forestall pain and death forever."[27] He wrote this volume as a philosopher, a medical ethics committee member, and as a son who was caring for his own father. Although there is not room here to unpack all of the principles that should guide us at the end of life, it is sufficient to say that the role of medicine is not to kill and that we should all recognize at the same time that medicine does have limits.[28]

What about Suffering?

Suffering is a compelling but complicated problem. It is important to understand it correctly because medicine is better at handling the

[27] Bill Davis, *Departing in Peace: Biblical Decision-Making at the End of Life* (Phillipsburg, NJ: P&R, 2017), 73.

[28] See the Christian Medical and Dental Associations' statement "On Medical Futility and the Good of the Patient" at https://cmda.org/policy-issues-home/position-statements/.

medical causes of suffering, but there are other causes that medicine cannot remedy. The late physician and bioethicist Eric Cassell helpfully observed that "although pain and suffering are closely identified in the minds of most people and in the medical literature, they are phenomenologically distinct."[29]

Strictly speaking, pain is a physical response to a noxious stimulus. Although that statement may lack feeling metaphorically, it is true. We are all aware of that physical response. Pain is something we feel, something we fear, and something we point to ("it hurts right here!"). It hurts, it aches, it stabs, it sears. Anyone who has been in the hospital has been asked, "On a scale of one to ten, how is your pain?" Or they have seen a set of six cartoon faces—the Wong-Baker Faces pain rating scale—with a face with tears at the one end and a happy face at the other end. Patients are asked to rank their pain accordingly. Having each patient rank his or her pain is both an acknowledgment that pain is a universal human experience, especially during illness, and that pain is idiosyncratic. That is, everyone experiences pain differently and to different degrees. Some have higher pain thresholds than others. Pain is personal and subjective. I cannot feel someone else's pain, though I can definitely relate to it because I have experienced a variety of pains myself.

It is such a profound experience that one of C. S. Lewis's classic volumes is *The Problem of Pain*. And in her brilliant reflections on the problem of pain, Elaine Scarry remarks, "For the person in pain, so incontestably and unnegotiably present is it that 'having pain' may come to be thought of as the most vibrant example of what it is to 'have certainty,' while for the other person it is so elusive that 'hearing about pain' may exist as the primary model of

---

[29] Eric Cassell, *The Nature of Suffering and the Goals of Medicine* (Oxford: Oxford University Press, 1991), 34.

what it is to 'have doubt.' Thus pain comes unsharably into our midst as at once that which cannot be denied and that which cannot be confirmed."[30]

The good news about pain is that medical science has found ways to manage pain so that, as Edmund Pellegrino observed, "With the optimum and judicious use of [pain management techniques], there are virtually no patients whose pain cannot be relieved."[31] Pain is treated by, first, understanding the cause of pain as much as possible and, then, by addressing the cause through some form of treatment (e.g., surgery) or through administration of analgesic medications. Medical science is getting better and better at managing pain.

Suffering, on the other hand, is as Dr. Cassell said is phenomenologically distinct. That is, it is a different animal so to speak. In a very helpful way, Daniel Sulmasy has offered what might be described as a taxonomy of suffering that demonstrates the variety of ways human beings suffer.

> Type I. Human beings can suffer as a result of our own moral evil without any intervening material occasion; examples include pangs of conscience, remorse, and guilt. This is the experience of personal finitude. A physician may feel guilty about having abandoned a patient and recognize his or her limited individual capacity for good. In penance, we confess our moral finitude as undermining our intrinsic dignity.

---

[30] Elaine Scarry, *The Body in Pain: The Making and Unmaking of the World* (Oxford: Oxford University Press, 1985), 4.

[31] Edmund Pellegrino, "Doctors Must Not Kill," *Journal of Clinical Ethics* 3, no. 2 (Summer 1992): 97, https://www.journals.uchicago.edu/doi/abs/10.1086/JCE199203202?journalCode=jce.

Type II. Human beings can suffer as a result of the moral evil of others without any intervening material occasion; examples include experiences of loneliness, hurt, and alienation. This is the experience of the moral finitude of others. If one were a patient, one might feel hurt by the cold and relatively inattentive manner in which one was treated by one's physician. No material would need serve as an intervening occasion of the suffering; the moral failure of the physician is sufficient cause. One recognizes that the world's love is finite.

Type III. Human beings can suffer as a result of the moral evil of self or of others mediated through material occasions of suffering. The long and horrible list of examples include self-mutilation, torture, assault, rape, poisoning, murder, war, and willful negligence. These are at once experiences of the moral finitude of others and of the material finitude of one's own person. Records and memories of "experiments" performed on Nazi prisoners provide especially egregious medical examples. More subtly, a physician's greed may lead to excessive use of medical technologies with attendant physical harm to some patients.

Type IV. A myriad of material occasions of human suffering that require no moral evil whatsoever—the central problems of medical suffering. Examples include fractured bones that result from landslides, inherited diseases like cystic-fibrosis and hemophilia, and the relentless commonplaces such as arthritis, diabetes, cancer, heart attacks, and strokes. These are personal experiences of material finitude. From the physician's perspective, they can also represent the physician's own experience of the finitude of medicine. Medicine does not grant immortality.

Mixed Types. Certainly there can be occasions of suffering that are, in part, directly material and, in part, the result of moral evil. Multiple combinations and permutations are possible. Examples could include a person with lung cancer who had a genetic predisposition but who also started smoking at an early age, in part because greedy tobacco company executives, motivated by a desire for profits, deliberately repressed evidence about the addictive nature of cigarettes and authorized an advertizing campaign aimed at teenagers. The bad genes are a contributing factor, but the teenager's decision to smoke and the business practices of the tobacco company played significant roles also.[32]

This taxonomy is an important reminder that (1) suffering is an existential experience of human beings as a particular kind of beings (see Neil Messer in chapter 2) and (2) although suffering may result from pain, once the pain has been treated, there may be other causes of suffering that analgesic medications cannot remedy. There is physical suffering, emotional suffering, spiritual suffering, familial suffering, and suffering that is the result of living in a fallen world where there are mean people and where there are natural disasters.

One of the problems of the PAS and euthanasia movement is that it tends to conflate pain and suffering. Instead of addressing

---

[32] Adapted from Ben Mitchell, PhD, and D. Joy Riley, MD, *Christian Bioethics: A Guide for Pastors, Health Care Professionals, and Families* (Nashville: B&H, 2014), 80–81. Mitchell and Riley cite Daniel P. Sulmasy, "Finitude, Freedom, and Suffering," in *Pain Seeking Understanding: Suffering, Medicine, and Faith*, ed. Margaret E. Mohrmann and Mark J. Hanson (Cleveland, TN: Pilgrim, 1999): 94–95.

the pain and then asking what other forms of suffering might need to be addressed, it offers the same remedy for both the pain and suffering: death. Yet, as Pellegrino observes, "Much of the suffering of dying patients comes from being subtly treated as nonpersons. The decisions to seek euthanasia is often an indictment against those who treat or care for the patient. If the emotional impediments to freedom and autonomy are removed, and pain is properly relieved, there is evidence that many would not choose euthanasia."[33]

Here is a strategic place for other types of caregivers, including counselors, social workers, families, pastors, and church members. Although they may not be able to remedy the physical causes of pain, they may be able to offer hope and point to remedies for the other types of suffering. Here is a place for churches to regain the legacy of their forebears who pioneered the hospital and hospice movements.

An inspiring example is Our Lady of Perpetual Help Cancer Home in Smyrna, Georgia, a suburb of Atlanta. Founded in 1939, the hospice ministry is staffed by the Hawthorne Dominican Sisters and is dedicated to the care of terminal cancer patients. The facility is open to those who cannot afford to pay for care. It is one of seven free homes for cancer patients operated by the nuns. It may be surprising, but the majority of patients are not Roman Catholic. The sisters are truly sisters of mercy. If the juggernaut of PAS and euthanasia is going to be stopped, it will require mercy ministries like Our Lady in the same way that, at the other end of life, pregnancy care centers have provided alternatives to elective abortion.

---

[33] Pellegrino, "Doctors Must Not Kill," 97.

5

Beyond Therapy

Looking into the future at goals pursuable with the aid of new biotechnologies enables us to turn a reflective glance at our own version of the human condition and the prospects now available to us (in principle) for a flourishing human life. For us today, assuming that we are blessed with good health and a sound mind, a flourishing human life is not a life lived with an ageless body or an untroubled soul, but rather a life lived in rhythmed time, mindful of time's limits, appreciative of each season and filled first of all with those intimate human relations that are ours only because we are born, age, replace ourselves, decline, and die—and know it. It is a life of aspiration, made possible by and born of experienced lack, of the disproportion between the transcendent longings of the soul and the limited capacities of our bodies and minds. It is a life that stretches towards some fulfillment to which our natural human soul has been oriented, and, unless we extirpate the source, will always be oriented. It is a life not of better genes and enhancing chemicals but of love and friendship, song and dance, speech and deed, working and learning, revering and worshipping.

—US President's Council on Bioethics,
Beyond Therapy, 2003

Better Than Well

Some people who are unhappy with the limitations of the human body believe the role of medicine is not only to heal and care but also to enhance human capabilities—to move beyond therapy to enhancement. As the title of philosopher Carl Elliott's volume puts it, we aim to be *Better Than Well*. Elliott suggests that this is a particularly American phenomenon evidenced by our consumerist penchant for self-improvement aids, drugs, and technologies. Given the human condition, is it really possible to be better than well? What would it mean to be better than well? How much better? And who decides what is better and what is not?

In 2003, the President's Council on Bioethics released a report called *Beyond Therapy: Biotechnology and the Pursuit of Happiness*.[1] The council was commissioned by George W. Bush in 2001 and was directed to "advise the President on bioethical issues that may emerge as a consequence of advances in biomedical science and technology."[2] Under the leadership of Leon Kass and, later, Edmund Pellegrino, the council published a number of extraordinary documents on a range of subjects including bioethics, biotechnology, cloning, stem cell research, aging, and artificial reproductive technologies. Their body of work was voluminous and profound in many ways.

---

[1] See *Beyond Therapy: Biotechnology and the Pursuit of Happiness* (Washington, DC: The President's Council on Bioethics, 2003), https://biotech.law.lsu.edu/research/pbc/reports/beyondtherapy/.

[2] Office of the Press Secretary, "Executive Order: Creation of the President's Council on Bioethics" press release, The White House: George W. Bush, November 28, 2001, https://georgewbush-whitehouse.archives.gov/news/releases/2001/11/20011128-13.html.

Beyond Therapy is essentially an exploration of the potential of biomedicine and biotechnology to extend human life, enhance human capabilities, and ostensibly contribute to human happiness. The means for becoming better than well encompass a host of technologies, including genetic modification. Julian Savulescu, the Chen Su Lan Centennial Professor in Medical Ethics and director of the Centre for Biomedical Ethics at National University of Singapore, is a proponent of genetic modification and believes that it must be used to enhance human beings. Savulescu has argued that "far from its being merely permissible, we have a moral obligation or moral reason to enhance ourselves and our children. Indeed, we have the same kind of obligation as we have to treat and prevent disease. Not only *can* we enhance, we *should* enhance."[3]

Although it is notoriously challenging to locate a bright line between therapy and enhancement, it is possible to draw lines. Sometimes the argument is made that everyone obviously favors human enhancements. The evidence offered is eyeglasses and hearing assist devices. Of course, a moment's reflection will identify these not as enhancements but as therapies that bring one's diminished capacities of sight and hearing up to (hopefully) species-typical norms. Likewise, the use of caffeine or modafinil to help one stay awake and alert are offered as examples. Although these do improve alertness, they do not do so beyond species-typical norms, and they have associated side effects that make their overuse harmful. Furthermore, they are temporary, effective only while being used. So, they are not enhancements

---

[3] Julian Savulescu, "New Breeds of Humans: The Moral Obligation to Enhance," *Reproductive BioMedicine* 10, Supp I (December 9, 2004): 38.

in the way that proponents of genetic and other enhancements generally mean.

Genetic Enhancement

Genetic enhancement refers to the aim of augmenting the human genome in such a way as either to enhance one person's species-typical capacities and abilities or, more often, to enhance the entire species *Homo sapiens*. There would be essentially three venues for manipulating human genetics. First, scientists might manipulate the human genetic material in germ cells—sperm and egg. We know, for example, that a cleft chin is a single-gene dominant trait passed from one generation to another through normal procreation. That gene could potentially be "turned off" in the germ cell so that trait would stop being expressed at some point in a family line. But why? Purely cosmetic reasons do not seem worthy of altering the genetic legacy of a family line. And there does not seem to be any pathology associated with a cleft chin. Likewise, any gene for a desirable trait could be "turned on" in the germ cells so that trait would more reliably occur in the next generation. "Desirable" is the key term. Why is it desirable to alter this or that gene? Whose values make it desirable?

In his volume *Choosing Children: Genes, Disability, and Design*, Kings College London philosopher-ethicist Jonathan Glover argues that we have a moral obligation to use genetic technology for therapeutic purposes and cannot rule out the possibility of enhancement.[4] Raising the specter of eugenics, in *Better Than Human*, Allen Buchanan has written, "Once we appreciate that some

---

[4] Jonathan Glover, *Choosing Children: Genes, Disability, and Design* (Oxford: Oxford University Press, 2008).

enhancements will bring broad social benefits, including increased productivity, we must abandon the comforting assumption that the risk of state-driven eugenics is a thing of the past."[5]

As Nicholas Agar has argued, however, the new eugenics should not be mandated by law as it was in Nazi Germany. It would be, according to the title of one of his books, *Liberal Eugenics*, a kinder, gentler eugenics encouraged by public opinion and shaming and through government incentives. Although in a subsequent volume, *Truly Human Enhancement: A Philosophical Defense of Limits*, he recognizes possible abuses, he nevertheless calls for genetic modification to be used to enhance human capacities.[6]

Julian Savulescu and his colleagues have argued not only that it is permissible to attempt to enhance human beings, even children, but also that it is morally obligatory once technology has afforded us the power to do so. Cognitive, mood, physical, lifespan, and even moral enhancements should be developed to make better humans, or even make people better than human.[7] Glover, Buchannan, Savulescu, and others do not want only to enhance individual children. That would be, among other things, too labor intensive. Rather, they want to enhance entire families of human beings and ultimately the entire species. This would have to be

---

[5] Allen Buchanan, *Better Than Human: The Promise and Perils of Enhancing Ourselves* (Oxford: Oxford University Press, 2011), 177.

[6] See Nicholas Agar, *Liberal Eugenics: In Defence of Human Enhancement* (Malden, MA: Blackwell, 2004); Nicholas Agar, *Truly Human Enhancement: A Philosophical Defense of Limits* (Cambridge: Massachusetts Institute of Technology, 2014).

[7] Julian Savulescu, Ruud ter Meulen, and Guy Kahane, eds., *Enhancing Human Capacities* (Hoboken, NJ: Wiley-Blackwell, 2011). A helpful commentary on the penchant for enhancement in American culture and medicine is Carl Elliot's, *Better Than Well: American Medicine Meets the American Dream* (New York: W. W. Norton, 2004).

done by manipulating the germline so that those traits would be passed from one generation to another.

Human germline modification is highly controversial and does not receive support through government funding in the United States and other countries. (But some jurisdictions, including the United Kingdom, are warming to the idea, at least with respect to the therapeutic uses of germline manipulation.[8]) In 2015, for instance, UNESCO's International Bioethics Committee called for a moratorium on germline genetic modification stating that "interventions on the human genome should be admitted only for preventive, diagnostic or therapeutic reasons and without enacting modifications for descendants" because germline modifications "jeopardize the inherent and therefore equal dignity of all human beings and renew eugenics."[9]

Second, the genetic material of a human embryo might be selected or manipulated using CRISPR or some other technology in vitro. Nick Bostrom, Oxford philosopher and former director of the Future of Humanity Institute, explores this kind of project in his volume, *Superintelligence: Paths, Dangers, Strategies*. Bostrom writes, "Embryo selection does not require a deep understanding of the causal pathways by which genes, in complicated interplay with environments, produce phenotypes: it requires only (lots of) data

[8] See Nuffield Council on Bioethics, *Genome Editing and Human Reproduction: Social and Ethical Issues* (London, 2018). Also available at https://www.nuffieldbioethics.org/publications/genome-editing-and-human-reproduction.

[9] "UNESCO Panel of Experts Calls for Ban on 'Editing' of Human DNA to Avoid Unethical Tampering with Hereditary Traits," UNESCO, October 5, 2015, last updated April 20, 2023, https://www.unesco.org/en/articles/unesco-panel-experts-calls-ban-editing-human-dna-avoid-unethical-tampering-hereditary-traits.

on the genetic correlates of the traits of interest."[10] In other words, because some traits are multifactorial—a combination of genetics and environmental factors—it might be difficult to identify the exact origins of something like IQ. But precision is not necessary if the genetic correlates of higher IQ among embryos could be identified through data analysis. So Bostrom maintains that with, say, 1,000 selection cycles, it might be possible to gain 24.3 IQ points among the embryos selected.[11] More sophisticated technologies, Bostrom believes, might result in even better results. Embryonic stem cell selection or synthetic biology might increase the potency and reliability of improving human cognition. One might avoid the manipulation of genetics altogether and move toward brain–computer interfaces, Bostrom speculates, but to explore that topic would take this chapter in a very different direction.

Life Extension

Another strategy for enhancement is life extension technologies. Not just extending the average human life span a few years, but indefinitely. Perhaps the premier popularizer of this idea is the Cambridge-based biogerontologist Aubrey de Grey, author of *Ending Aging: The Rejuvenation Breakthroughs That Could Reverse Human Aging in Our Lifetime.*[12] As the title indicates, de Grey's mission is not to eliminate the deleterious pathologies sometimes associated with aging such as muscle loss, memory loss, frailty, and

---

[10] Nick Bostrom, *Superintelligence: Paths, Dangers, Strategies* (Oxford: Oxford University Press, 2014), 37.

[11] Bostrom, 45.

[12] Aubrey de Grey and Michael Rae, *Ending Aging: The Rejuvenation Breakthroughs That Could Reverse Human Aging in Our Lifetime* (New York: St. Martin's, 2007).

eventually, death. His aim is to eliminate aging altogether. In other words, he is what is sometimes called a proponent of radical life extension or an immortalist.

To promote anti-aging technologies, de Grey and his colleagues have established the "Methuselah Mouse Prize," or MPrize, for developments in life extension research.[13] The current mission of the foundation that awards the prize is "to make 90 the new 50 by 2030." Make no mistake, however: this is merely a preliminary goal. Immortality through technology is the end game (no pun intended). "The right to live as long as you choose is the world's most fundamental right," claims de Grey.[14]

Aubrey de Grey is not alone in his quest for immortality. George Church, a Harvard and MIT geneticist, believes that aging can be "cured" by targeted gene therapies. He and his colleague, John Oliver, co-founded Rejuvenate Bio to do just that, first in dogs then in humans. Church is also coauthor of *Regenesis: How Synthetic Biology Will Reinvent Nature and Ourselves.*[15] Synthetic biology uses multiple biotechnologies to design and develop novel genes and other biological parts not found in nature. The aim is to increase human intelligence, memory, physical strength, and other capacities—eventually leading to the elimination of aging. In the meantime, it might be possible, Church thinks, to bring some species

---

[13] It is called the mouse prize because medical research is typically done first on mice since they are the species best able in most cases to model the way drugs will interact with human biology. See the Methuselah Foundation's website at https://www.mfoundation.org/.

[14] Sherwin Nuland, "Do You Want to Live Forever?: Aubrey de Grey Thinks He Knows How to Defeat Aging. He's Brilliant, but Is He Nuts?," *MIT Technology Review*, February 1, 2005, https://www.technologyreview.com/2005/02/01/231686/do-you-want-to-live-forever/.

[15] George Church and Ed Regis, *Regenesis: How Synthetic Biology Will Reinvent Nature and Ourselves* (New York: Basic Books, 2014).

like the woolly mammoth back from the dead. Americans are basically divided on some of these goals. A 2022 Pew Research Center Report found the following responses to a variety of enhancements:

> Cognitive enhancement: Nearly half of Americans (47 percent) say they would be at least somewhat excited about techniques that allow some people to "far more quickly and accurately process information."
>
> Auditory enhancement: More Americans say they would be excited (47 percent) than concerned (24 percent) about techniques that allow some people "to hear sounds far beyond what a typical person can hear today." About three-in-ten (29 percent) say they would respond to such developments with an equal mix of excitement and concern.
>
> Physical strength: Improvements to physical capabilities garner a similar response: 44 percent of Americans say they would be excited about new techniques that would allow some people greatly increased strength for lifting heavy objects, 27 percent say they would be concerned and 28 percent would have an equal mix of both reactions.
>
> Visual enhancement: 41 percent of Americans say they would be at least somewhat excited by developments that would enhance human vision, allowing some people to see shapes and patterns in crowded spaces to a degree far beyond what is typical today. A larger share say either that they are concerned by (28 percent) or that they have a mixed reaction to this possible enhancement (31 percent).
>
> Radical life extension: 41 percent say they would greet the possibility of a major change to the human lifespan with

> excitement, a concept called radical life extension because it would slow the aging process and allow the average person to live decades longer. Three-in-ten say they would have an equal mix of positive and negative response to this prospect, and a similar share (29 percent) would primarily be concerned.[16]

Some Common Ground

Many of the individuals involved in the genetic enhancement and radical life extension projects are part of a philosophical/scientific movement known at transhumanism. One popular media source for education by the transhumanist movement is the website Humanity+. The mission of Humanity+ is stated there: "We want people to be better than well. Humanity+ supports the development of high-impact technology to make beneficial futures attainable. We focus on science, technology, culture, and social issues."[17] Although not all immortalists or longtermists identify with transhumanism, their approach to aging, life extension, and the future of medicine follow one another closely. Some longtermists may not know transhumanism at all, but as theologian Jacob Shatzer has argued, many Americans are naïve transhumanists because they are uncritical early adopters of technologies that promise to make us better than well.[18]

---

[16] Lee Rainie et al., "5. What Americans Think about Possibilities ahead for Human Enhancement," Pew Research Center, March 17, 2022, https://www.pewresearch.org/internet/2022/03/17/what-americans-think-about-possibilities-ahead-for-human-enhancement/.

[17] "Our Mission," humanityplus.org, accessed October 14, 2024, https://www.humanityplus.org/about.

[18] See Jacob Shatzer, *Transhumanism and the Image of God: Today's Technology and the Future of Christian Discipleship* (Lisle, IL: IVP Academic, 2019).

Uncritical early adoption has become what communications professor Quentin Schultze referred to as one of the habits of the high-tech heart.[19] It is one of the reasons there are long lines around the Apple store every time a bright, shiny, new digital bobble is released. We almost cannot resist, even if we might find out later that the new technology brings unanticipated burdens with it.[20]

Transhumanists and Christians may share some common ground but disagree on the means to the end. It is worth considering these points of common concern. First, both transhumanists and Christians find human suffering to be a lamentable aspect of the human condition. Through the ages, Christians have worked to relieve human suffering through acts of mercy, kindness, and care. As we have seen already in this book, Christians have been at the forefront of caring for the most vulnerable, building hospitals, and serving in hospice work. But transhumanists want to address the problem of suffering by ultimately escaping our embodied existence in a posthuman future.

Second, both Christians and transhumanists long for immortality. But is it possible, or even desirable, to extend human life indefinitely? In a brilliant essay, Leon Kass has offered an insightful set of diagnostic questions on this broad goal of immortality. In the essay, "L'Chaim and Its Limits: Why Not Immortality?"[21] Kass uses

---

[19] Quentin Schultze, *Habits of the High-Tech Heart: Living Virtuously in the Information Age* (Ada, MI: Baker, 2004).

[20] See, for instance, Albert Borgmann, *Power Failure: Christianity in the Culture of Technology* (Ada, MI: Baker, 2003): Craig Gay, *Modern Technology and the Human Future: A Christian Appraisal* (Lisle, IL: IVP Academic, 2018.

[21] Leon R. Kass, "L'Chaim and Its Limits: Why Not Immortality?" *First Things* 113 (May 2001): 17–24, https://www.firstthings.com/article/2001/05/lchaim-and-its-limits-why-not-immortality.

the traditional Jewish toast of celebration, "L'Chaim" (To Life!), as a heuristic device to assist us in examining our naïve assumptions about living forever in this fallen world. Clearly, we favor life, but should we put our hopes in limitless life? "How *much* longer life is a blessing for an individual?" asks Kass, "Could longer, healthier life be less satisfying?" Are there ways our finitude might be good for us? Consider several diagnostic questions:

> If the human life span were increased even by only twenty years, would the pleasures of life increase proportionately? Would professional tennis players really enjoy playing 25 percent more games of tennis? Would Don Juans of our world feel better about having seduced 1,250 women rather than 1,000? Having experienced the joys and tribulations of raising a family until the last had left for college, how many parents would like to extend the experience by another ten years? Likewise, those whose satisfaction comes from climbing the career ladder might well ask what there would be to do for fifteen years after one had been CEO of Microsoft, a member of Congress, or the President of Harvard for a quarter of a century? Even less clear are the additions to personal happiness from more of the same of the less pleasant and less fulfilling activities in which so many of us are engaged so much of the time. It seems to be as the poet says: "We move and ever spend our lives amid the same things, and not by any length of life is any new pleasure hammered out."[22]

I will list others for reflection:

---

[22] Kass, "L'Chaim and Its Limits."

> Could life be serious or meaningful without the limit of mortality?
>
> Does not our appreciation of the beautiful turn in part on our brevity of life?
>
> How deeply would one deathless "human" being love another?
>
> Would immortal human beings need courage, endurance, greatness of soul, generosity, and devotion to justice to rise above our mere creatureliness?
>
> Does not immortality become a kind of oblivion? The price of immortality is the loss of our humanity.

These are profound existential questions. As we saw in chapter 2, any theological account of human health, disease, and medicine must begin by recognizing the particular kind of creatures we are. Against the utopian vision of transhumanism, there is no real reason to believe that, even with some enhancements, human beings will be able to live forever in our incarnate condition.

Our fallen human bodies were not designed to live forever. And in a fallen world of human frailty, injustice, violence, oppression, and other vices, immortality would be a living hell. As the preacher says, there is "a time to give birth and a time to die" (Eccl 3:2). As the apostle Paul wrote to the Corinthian believers, immortality will be our future, but not in this jar of clay (2 Cor 4:7) or earthly tent (2 Cor 5:1–4). They are allusions to the temporary nature of our carbon-based embodiment. This is the groaning stage. Yet "we know that if our earthly tent we live in is destroyed, we have a building from God, an eternal dwelling in the heavens, not made with hands" (v. 1). The frail, temporary tent of a body will be replaced by a strong, durable, permanent building of a body, made for us by God.

Christians and transhumanists agree that immortality is desirable, but they differ profoundly on both the nature of that immortality and the means to achieve it. For Christians, it is not a posthuman future we desire but a fully human future revealed to us in the person and body of the resurrected Christ, Jesus of Nazareth. Hippocratic, especially Christian-Hippocratic medicine, is pledged by the medical covenant to treat human suffering for the benefit of the patient and not doing harm by eliminating her humanity. Christians have been promised that suffering of every sort will one day be relieved by transfiguration, not transhumanism.[23]

Finally, both transhumanists and Christians appreciate the benefits of technology. Grounded in the mandate to "be fruitful and increase in number; fill the earth and subdue it. Rule over the fish in the sea and the birds in the sky and over every living creature that moves on the ground" (Gen 1:28 NIV). This text is what is sometimes called the dominion or stewardship mandate. The Judeo-Christian tradition provides rich impetus for technological invention. God put his image-bearers in a garden "to work it and take care of it" (2:15 NIV), to classify the natural order (Gen 2:20), and to sustain themselves, after the fall, by the sweat of their brows (3:17). Later generations of humans made tools (4:22), planted vineyards (9:20), made weapons (10:9), and built great cities

---

[23] See Kimbell Kornu, "Transfiguration, Not Transhumanism: Suffering as Human Enhancement," *Heythrop Journal* 63 (2022): 926–39. See also, Renee Mirkes, "Transhumanist Medicine: Can We Direct Its Power to the Service of Human Dignity?" *Linacre Quarterly* 86, no. 1 (2019): 115–26.

(v. 11). *Homo sapiens* (human knowers) are by their very nature and calling *Homo faber* (human fabricators). The history of science and technology is replete with the names of Christians who saw it as their calling to be cocreators and innovators: Francis Bacon, Galileo Galilei, Johannes Kepler, Charles Babbage, Gregor Mendel, and thousands of others up to today's Francis Collins, co-discoverer of the gene for cystic fibrosis.

Obviously, transhumanists are technological optimists. And this may be part of the problem, an optimism that borders on, and sometimes commits itself to, technological utopianism. We should be reminded that the literal meaning of the word *utopia* is "no place." In his award-winning volume, *Homo Deus*, historian Yuval Noah Harari declares:

> *Homo sapiens* is likely to upgrade itself step by step, merging with robots and computers in the process, until our descendants look back and realise that they are no longer the kind of animal that wrote the Bible, built the Great Wall of China and laughed at Charlie Chaplin's antics. This will not happen in a day, or a year. Indeed, it is already happening right now, through innumerable mundane actions. Every day millions of people decide to grant their smartphone a bit more control over their lives or try a new and more effective antidepressant drug. In pursuit of health, happiness, and power, humans will gradually change first one of their features and then another, and another, until they will no longer be human.[24]

He maintains that

[24] Yuval Noah Harari, *Homo Deus: A Brief History of Tomorrow* (New York: Harper, 2017), 49.

> these powers are far more potent than steam and the telegraph, and they will not be used mainly for the production of food, textiles, vehicles and weapons. The main products of the twenty-first century will be bodies, brains and minds, and the gap between those who know how to engineer bodies and brains and those who do not will be wider than the gap between Dickens's Britain and the Madhi's Sudan. Indeed, it will be bigger than the gap between Sapiens and Neanderthals. In the twenty-first century, those who ride the train of progress will acquire divine abilities of creation and destruction, while those left behind will face extinction.[25]

Harari's prediction is bracing, to be sure. I suppose time will tell whether this is a utopia or a dystopia.

Transgenderism

In *Better Than Well*, Carl Elliott introduces his readers to a group who call themselves "Amputee Wannabes." These are individuals who voluntarily would choose to have an amputation of a perfectly healthy limb or body part. The fetish is called apotemnophilia or body identity integrity dysphoria (BIID). The disorder is relatively rare but, says Elliott, "not *nearly* as rare as one might think."[26] According to the International Classification of Diseases group of the World Health Organization, BIID is "an intense and persistent desire to become physically disabled in a significant way

---

[25] Harari, 275.

[26] Carl Elliott, *Better Than Well: American Medicine Meets the American Dream* (New York: W. W. Norton, 2004), 208.

(e.g., a major limb amputation, paraplegia, blindness) accompanied by persistent discomfort or intense negative feelings about one's current body configuration or functioning."[27] Estimates are that there are about one thousand sufferers of this disorder worldwide.[28] Elliott also recounts the story of a surgeon in Scotland who, in 2000, amputated the legs of two patients at their request and would have "treated" a third patient had the health authority not stopped him.[29]

Is medicine—are doctors—morally obligated to put a patient at unnecessary risk to remove a healthy limb just because a patient makes a so-called autonomous request? If so, where does the obligation come from? Might it not be the case instead that the patient's autonomy should be questioned? Even if it is viewed to be an autonomous request, should medicine's first ethical principle—"do no harm"—be mutilated along with the patient's body?

Both our intuition and, for the time being at least, the psychiatric community see BIID as a psychological disorder. At the same time, however, the transgender phenomenon—including trans surgery—has been growing in the US and Europe. Is trans surgery a "treatment" or an abuse of patients and a violation of the Hippocratic covenant? These are important ethical questions for consideration.

Transgenderism is one of the latest mile markers in the long march of the rise of the modern self that had its origins in the

---

[27] ICD-11 for Mortality and Morbidity Statistics, "6C21 Body Integrity Dysphoria," 2024, https://icd.who.int/browse/2024-01/mms/en#256572629.

[28] Michelle Orange, "If One Part Suffers: The Enigma of Body Integrity Dysphoria," *Harper's Magazine* (January 2024). Also available at https://harpers.org/archive/2024/01/if-one-part-suffers/?ref=thebrowser.com.

[29] Elliott, *Better Than Well*, 208.

Enlightenment. Prior to the Enlightenment, human persons were understood to be made in the image of God as gifts to be received from the Creator. Today, the human person has become a naked "self"—a do-it-yourself project to be created in one's own image. Since the sexual revolution of the 1960s, the self has been increasingly sexualized. Simultaneously, sex has been politicized through culture wars over contraception and abortion. The result is the modern self—a single, solitary, atomistic, and sexualized self as a self-governing domain.

Explosive growth in the areas of technology, consumerism, and entertainment over the past three centuries has changed not only what we do but how we think (epistemology), expanding our epistemological horizons for both good and ill. In the last century, medical technologies have made possible what was once unthinkable, including the contraceptive pill that has sundered the connection between sexual intimacy and procreation. The sexualized self was freed from some of the consequences of casual sex.

As the individual came to perceive him-self or her-self as ruler of his or her personal domain, consumerism and entertainment captured the imagination, opening the possibility of sexual experimentation, gender fluidity, and even alterations of the human body. Where once limits were framed by biology, now they are framed by technology and the imagination. Where once trans clothing and makeup were the only available options, now chemical and surgical interventions make possible the remaking of the sexualized self, even if that means mutilating the biological self. Today that revolution is promoted through every form of social media. Television programs such as *Chad* (2021) and films such as *The Crying Game* (1990), *Boys Do not Cry* (1999), and *TransAmerica* (2005) have made disordered love romantic, even heroic.

Gender Identity and the Modern Self

Sadly, in our cultural context people are taught that their psychology is the source of their sexual identity. They are taught that if their psychological gender identity differs from their birth sex, they should attempt to conform their body to their gender identity through the use of styles of dress, chemical interventions, and even surgical alterations of the body. On the contrary, Holy Scripture, human biology, and medical science teach us that our body—specifically our gonads—is a gift of our creatureliness to be received with gratitude. The body is the source of our sexual identity, and we should bring our minds into conformity with our bodies. Body identity dysphoria is after all, a "dis-order." Yet as one historian of science has put it, in our culture:

> Trans rights activism demands the endorsement of a set of contestable "facts": that gender identity is innate and objectively known even by children, while sex is a social construction; that trans identification never arises from psychological distress; that the sudden rise in trans identification, including marked changes in sex and age demographics, is satisfactorily explained by greater trans visibility and acceptance; that regret over medical transition is rare; and that blockers are safe and reversible, promote mental health and avert suicide risks. It is a take-it-or-leave-it package deal, and to question any part of it is to be "anti-trans."[30]

---

[30] Cordelia Fine, "Building on Sands of Ignorance: How the Tavistock Trust's Gender Identity Clinic Failed Its Patients," *Times Literary Supplement*, March 17, 2023, https://www.the-tls.co.uk/articles/time-to-think-tavistock-clinic-hannah-barnes-book-review-cordelia-fine/.

Consumer Medicine and the Modern Self

Nowhere has the autonomous self become more omnipresent than in modern medicine. Admittedly, Western, Hippocratic medicine was sometimes characterized by an overweening paternalism. The doctor was always right. But the ascent of the modern self has eclipsed physician paternalism to such an extent that now patient autonomy is the guiding principle of medical decision-making. The patient is always right, and medicine is just another consumer good. The bible of contemporary medical ethics, *Principles of Biomedical Ethics* by Tom L. Beauchamp and James F. Childress, lists four basic ethical principles that are to be used in making medical decisions: respect for autonomy, beneficence, non-maleficence, and justice, with the latter three primarily used to optimize patient autonomy.[31] The autonomous self now drives decisions for elective abortion, euthanasia, reproductive technologies, and the whole range of medical procedures, including transgender medications and surgeries. The question must be asked of gender transition protocols, How does the right to self-determination force the moral move to co-opting physicians and medicine to, as it were, kill one's sex in favor of one's idiosyncratic gender construct (e.g., as a "furry")?

Data Vacuum and the Language of Therapy

Because the trans phenomenon is relatively recent, there are no thirty- or forty-year longitudinal studies for reliable data.

---

[31] See Tom L. Beauchamp and James F. Childress, *Principles of Biomedical Ethics*, 8th ed. (Oxford: Oxford University Press, 2019).

Because the study of sex, gender, and identity is so highly politicized, even studies published in reputable scientific journals may be biased in favor of the individual and the notion of the body as personal property.

Gender dysphoria is a condition where one experiences anxiety, confusion, or a disconnect between one's sexual identity and one's gender identity. This is sometimes called gender identity disorder or incongruence. The human person is dis-ordered and dis-integrated through gender dysphoria. Genuine treatment for gender dysphoria includes counseling to help someone bring their gender identity into conformity with their biological sex, to reintegrate themselves. We should not deny that gender dysphoria is real, but we have to contest some of the suppositions that underwrite many of the medical protocols.

Language Matters

Both the scientific literature and popular media surrounding gender dysphoria and transgenderism use the language of "treatment" and "therapy" to refer to chemical and surgical interventions to attempt to transition one's sexual identity into one's gender identity (i.e., to conform one's biology to one's psychology). To call those interventions a treatment or therapy may unwittingly lead to the conclusion that one's biological sex is a disease or illness to be treated. This is not the case. Biological sex is a gift of God. Instead of treating the dysphoria, both chemical and surgical interventions are increasingly on offer as a work-around, as it were. Understanding those procedures, including their risks and their costs, is important in counseling those who may be considering them.

Puberty Blockers

A now infamous study of children treated at the Tavistock Gender Clinic in the United Kingdom found that the majority of children in the study did not resume puberty and "that children's bone density and normal growth flatlined with puberty blockers as compared to their peers, and participants reported no improvement in their psychological well-being. The findings support a growing body of evidence showing the harm and irreparable damage of experimental medical treatments for children with gender dysphoria."[32]

In December 2020, the UK High Court issued a ruling requiring doctors to seek a court order before administering puberty blockers to children under sixteen years of age. Controversy over "gender-affirming care" finally led to the shuttering of the Tavistock Gender Clinic in 2023. Despite claims that the science is settled, the clinical evidence is still largely inconclusive. National health bodies in Europe, including Sweden, France, and Finland, have all called for far greater caution in the use of puberty blockers.

More recently, the National Health Service in the UK released an independent review of gender identity services for children and young people. Headed by Hilary Cass, one of the most highly respected pediatricians in the world with more than thirty years of experience, the Cass Review offers conclusions based on extensive evidence, including eight systematic literature reviews, surveys of clinics across Europe, and interviews with over 1,000 patients, families, and clinicians in the field. The Cass Review maintains that exploration of gender identity is a completely natural process

---

[32] Mary Jackson, "Study: Effects of Puberty-blockers Can Last a Lifetime," *World* (December 18, 2020). Also available at https://wng.org/roundups/study-effects-of-puberty-blockers-can-last-a-lifetime-1617220389.

during childhood and adolescence, rarely requiring clinical intervention. After a systematic and independent analysis of the existing research, the Cass Reviews concludes, among other things, that puberty blockers should never be prescribed to patients under eighteen years of age, except in very rare circumstances. Furthermore, the report supports the idea that a medical solution may not be the best means for addressing gender distress.[33]

Detransitioning

There is strong evidence to suggest that many individuals who have undergone some form of "treatment" for gender dysphoria experience "trans regret." As many as 20 to 30 percent of individuals discontinue hormone treatment within a few years. Evidence suggests that the number of detransitioners may increase. These and other data have led many in the health-care and psychiatric community to reconsider the safety, efficacy, and risks of gender transition protocols, especially among children.[34]

---

[33] Final Report, *Cass Review*, https://cass.independent-review.uk/home/publications/final-report/.

[34] See Christina M. Roberts et al., "Continuation of Gender-affirming Hormones among Transgender Adolescents and Adults," *Journal of Clinical Endocrinology and Metabolism* 107, no. 9 (August 18, 2022): e3937–43; https://pubmed.ncbi.nlm.nih.gov/35452119; Michael S. Irwig, "Detransition Among Transgender and Gender-Diverse People—An Increasing and Increasingly Complex Phenomenon," *Journal of Clinical Endocrinology and Metabolism* 107, no. 10 (October 2022): e4261–62, https://academic.oup.com/jcem/article/107/10/e4261/6604653?login=false. For testimonies of women who have detransitioned, see the documentary film *Detransition Diaries* produced by the Center for Bioethics and Culture, https://cbc-network.org/film-detransition-diaries/; see also Jennifer Lahl and Kallie Fell, *The Detransition Diaries* (San Francisco: Ignatius, 2024).

Irreversibility and Mortality

It is crucial to remind individuals who are considering transition surgery that these modifications to the body are not reversible. If someone does detransition, one will continue to live with the changes made to the body to alter secondary sex characteristics. A person may attempt to hide or mask those changes, but they cannot be reversed.

Furthermore, in one of the largest studies to date, researchers estimate that trans people were nearly twice as likely to die over the period of the study as their non-trans counterparts. The report concluded that "trans people in our study had significantly higher rates of mortality at nearly every age than their non-trans counterparts. We also found significant variation of mortality risk within subpopulations of trans people, with the trans feminine/nonbinary and trans unclassified groups being at the greatest risk of mortality."[35]

Since every human being is made in God's image, including those individuals experiencing gender dysphoria, every human being is worthy of respect, love, and care. Care, however, must be consistent with an accurate diagnosis. Gender dysphoria is not a pathology of diseased or dysfunctional body parts (breasts, secondary sex characteristics, etc.). Appropriate medical care, therefore, should not include hormones to suppress puberty, estrogen to imitate female secondary sex characteristics in males, testosterone to imitate male sex characteristics in females, and surgical removal of breast, genitals, or other physical features. Healthy bodies should not be mutilated for psychological reasons.

---

[35] Landon D. Hughes et al., "Differences in All-Cause Mortality among Transgender and Non-Transgender People Enrolled in Private Insurance," *Demography* 59, no. 3 (June 1, 2022): 1023–43, https://www.ncbi.nlm.nih.gov/pmc/articles/PMC9195044/#S17title.

6

Conclusion: The Way of Medicine

The essence of humanistic ethics is this: particular features of illness diminish and obstruct a patient's capacity to live a specifically human existence to the fullest. These features created a relationship of inherent inequality between two human beings: one a physician, the other a patient. That inequality must be removed as fully as possible before the humanity of the patient can be restored. The obligation to restore the patient's humanity is intrinsic in the relationship physicians assume when they "profess" medicine. Specific obligations are derived from the "profession"—an active assumption by the physician as a free person entering a relationship with another person. These obligations transcend any responsibilities, rights, or privileges physicians may feel were conferred upon them by the degrees they possess.

—Edmund Pellegrino, *The Philosophy of Medicine Reborn*

Every time I mention to a physician or nurse that our health-care system is broken, I not only get nods of agreement; I get a litany of complaints. These are not weak-kneed softies; they are excellent, experienced, courageous, and virtuous doctors and nurses. Yet they are completely exhausted by the demands of the status quo (remember, that is Latin for "the mess we're in").

What Is the Way Forward?

One reason I have stayed with my current internist for primary care is because on our first appointment he described himself as a curmudgeon. He is not. But he went on to tell me that he did not use a scribe for notetaking or have a nurse practitioner see patients instead of himself. He takes his own notes by hand and dictates them himself after the visit. If he cannot see me for some reason, he will refer me to a physician colleague. He is a very good medical professional who is worried about the erosion of the embodied relationship between a physician and patient and the way that relationship is under threat by the pressures of third-party payers, drug companies, medical technology, and the primacy of efficiency (the fifteen-minute-per-patient rule) as the value that seems to trump nearly all other concerns.

Efficiency is sometimes a helpful metric, but it is a very poor master. Efficiency promises us we can get more done, faster than ever before. All things being equal (which they seldom are), efficiency is fine when making widgets in a factory or crunching data in a digital spreadsheet. Efficiency, however, can be inappropriate and even pathological in some contexts. For instance, we do not measure friendship, parenthood, or other human relationships by their efficiency. What would it mean for a child to say to her mother, "You're the most efficient mother a daughter could want"? That is either a category mistake, because that is not how we assess the value of motherhood, or some kind of complaint. Motherhood, fatherhood, and friendship are very inefficient when done well.

Education is very inefficient when done well. Think about the Oxford and Cambridge tutorial systems, for instance. There is nothing efficient about a single professor sitting in an office while a single student reads his or her paper out loud, only to have it critiqued and to have the student sent off either to revise the paper or begin the research for the next one. Although inefficient, it is a highly effective means of education. It is embodied, personal, improvisational, and human in a way an "efficient" lecture to an audience of 250 in an auditorium or webinar simply cannot be. Since there are few more intimate relationships than that between a physician and patient—someone who is a healer and someone who is ill—should we be surprised that efficiency is not helping? Needle pricks, lab values, and algorithms may be useful, but at the end of the day, medicine is an inherently "*person*-al" practice. One person caring for another person using technologies as tools and institutional structures as aids, but neither as masters.

Realistically, we cannot overhaul our health-care system completely. It might be unwise to do so in fact. There are so many layers, and the domino effect would be almost beyond anyone's prognostic capacities. But that does not mean we are stuck with the status quo. There are things that can be done to restore a robust morality to the ethics of medicine. Here are a few that flow from the previous chapters.

Rehabilitation of Christian-Hippocratism

Whether it is called Christian-Hippocratism or not, physicians and patients can order their respective roles around the principles, values, and virtues of the medical covenant. Christian-Hippocratism is life-affirming without being vitalist. That is, the tradition prohibits a physician from performing abortions or euthanasia on demand. At the same time, the tradition recognizes that prolonging human life indefinitely is not the aim of medicine. When medicine has done what it can and should do for the sake of the patient's health and flourishing, that is good enough. When there is nothing more that medicine can and should do, it is time to pivot to palliation.

Medical education should obviously be strong on the science of medicine. By its nature, medical education should also be robust in the art of medicine. At the same time, medical education neglects the philosophical/theological dimensions of health care outlined in this book at its own peril and at the peril of patients. As we learned from Paul Ramsey in the epigraph in chapter 2, "The doctor makes decisions as an expert but also as a man among men; and his patient is a human being coming to his birth or to his death, or being rescued from illness or injury in between."[1] This is an existentially profound reality that demands our best philosophical and theological reflection. Yet reflection is not sufficient. Action must also attend the reflection. Someone's life and health hang in the balance.

Rehydration of Professionalism

Along with the science, art, and philosophical foundation, medical ethics must also rehydrate medical professionalism. Professionalism, as we have seen in this book, is about far more than etiquette. It is about the nature of the vocational calling itself and the way professionals are formed as professionals. Curlin and Toleffsen argue that

[1] Paul Ramsey, *The Patient as Person: Explorations in Medical Ethics* (New Haven, CT: Yale University Press, 1970), xi.

"for practitioners of medicine, then, the central obligation . . . is clear: to act reasonably to preserve and restore the patient's health and to refuse to act otherwise."[2] And this must be the case despite the pressures of consumerism, bureaucracy, and efficiency.

According to Pellegrino, contemporary cultural pressures tempt physicians to become mere functionaries: "Complexities in the physician-patient relationship, introduced by the capabilities and the pluralism of values in a democratic society, are accentuated by the depersonalization inherent in the growing institutionalization and bureaucratization of the medical encounter."[3] The result is a shrunken humanity, of both the professional and of the patient.

Nussbaum uses the helpful metaphor of the physician as the captain of a ship. What physicians can do, he says, "is think of ourselves as something more than technicians in control of the body. At times, we can be like gardeners, teachers, servants, or witnesses to the people we meet as patients. . . . There is another role for a physician that also makes medical practice worthwhile, that of a ship's captain."[4] This metaphor is from Basil of Caesarea, the founder of the first public hospital in AD 369. It had three hundred beds and was built by the church. St. Basil wrote about the physician, "As we entrust the helm to the pilot in the art of navigation, but implore God that we may end our voyage unharmed by the

---

[2] Farr Curlin and Christopher Tollefsen, *The Way of Medicine: Ethics and the Healing Profession* (Notre Dame, IN: University of Notre Dame Press, 2021), 185.

[3] Edmund D. Pellegrino, *The Philosophy of Medicine Reborn: A Pellegrino Reader* (Notre Dame, IN: University of Notre Dame Press, 2008), 92.

[4] Abraham M. Nussbaum, *The Finest Traditions of My Calling: One Physician's Search for the Renewal of Medicine* (New Haven, CT: Yale University Press, 2016), 254.

perils of the sea, so also, when reason allows, we call in the doctor, but we do not leave off hoping in God."[5] Nussbaum's commentary on Basil is illuminating:

> Illness is not algebra, but a journey into dark waters. When you are ill, you need a captain, and I take Basil to mean that a physician can be our captain during an illness without taking authority for our lives outside that illness. If physicians are this kind of captain, we can trust their expertise during specific times of need without allowing them control over our bodies and lives. Physicians who understand themselves as this kind of captain would acknowledge that as death nears their role recedes. Instead of spending our last moments being examined by teams of physicians, residents, and students, we might thank the physician-captain for his or her assistance and turn to others for help with death. We could trust physicians to diagnose illnesses, prescribe treatments, and respond to complications, but we would finally trust other people to decide the meaning of our bodies and lives.[6]

Chastening of Consumerism in Medicine

In a very insightful editorial in *The American Journal of Medicine*, Salvatore Mangione, Brian Mandell, and Stephen Post push back against the consumerism of contemporary medicine with the

---

[5] St. Basil the Great, *The Fathers of the Church: St. Basil Ascetical Works*, trans. M. Monica Wagner, *The Fathers of the Church: A New Translation*, vol. 9 (Washington, DC: Catholic University of America Press, 1962), 336.

[6] Nussbaum, *Finest Traditions of My Calling*, 255–56.

reminder that "words matter." Specifically, they point out how describing physicians as "providers" undermines the true aim and perception of medicine. Traditionally, doctors have been viewed as much more than dispensers of goods and services. Worse, the term was used historically to debase certain members of the profession.

The Nazis were the first to use the term *provider* to refer to physicians. During the 1930s, when the Nazis came to power, nearly 50 percent of the 1,243 pediatricians in Hitler's Reich were deemed to be Jewish. To humiliate them—and eventually all German physicians of Jewish descent—the Reich revoked their licenses and downgraded them to "Krankenbehandler," or "providers." The embarrassing title was printed on their signs, their prescription pads, and their stationery from then on. It was a way to put them in their place.

No one would argue that in our day "health-care provider" is meant to be derisive, but it does carry a certain baggage. As Mangione, Mandell, and Post say, "Medicine is not immune and has seemingly adopted the corporate-speak of 'customer (patient) satisfaction,' 'stakeholders,' 'enterprise,' 'deliverables.'"[7] Characterizing doctors as mere providers de-emphasizes their professional status, training, and responsibility. Although they admit that this was not the intention, perhaps "the *language game* of today's medicine is the latest attempt to industrialize our relationship with the patient by turning it into another financial transaction. Like Orwell's Newspeak, this will define how the public sees us and how we ultimately see ourselves. Hence, it should be resisted."[8]

---

[7] Salvatore Mangione, Brian F. Mandell, and Stephen G. Post, "The Language Game: We Are Physicians, Not Providers," *American Journal of Medicine* 134, no. 12 (December 2021): 1445, https://www.amjmed.com/article/S0002-9343(21)00442-3/pdf.

[8] Mangione, Mandell, and Post, 1446.

Realism about Autonomy

As I and others have argued, the pendulum has swung from physician to paternalism to patient autonomy. Radical patient autonomy not only feeds the consumerism and PSM of contemporary medicine; it also underestimates the impact of illness and disease on the patient. Although not all illness renders a patient unable to make reasonable decisions for himself or herself, illness makes a patient vulnerable in ways that sometimes compromise self-determination.

One of the ethical and legal canons of medical ethics is the doctrine of informed consent. "The patients' rights movement and the doctrine of informed consent," suggest Curlin and Tollefsen, "rightly qualified and delimited physicians' commitment to pursue health. Out of respect for the persons they serve, physicians are to act only with the permission of their patients. Because health is neither the only nor highest good, patients are authorized to situate that good in relation to other concerns such as not to be overburdened by medical technology."[9] In other words, patients have a right to determine what happens to their bodies within the range of their own values and life goals. Patients can, and do, refuse treatments. In fact, to treat a competent patient against his or her will is a form of battery in the law.

Note, however, that although medicine recognizes the importance of consent, it also calls on physicians to render sufficient education for the patient to be informed about treatment options. This is another example of the illuminating nature of the dancing metaphor. Let us say a patient is diagnosed with osteoporosis. Although it is not required, it is more than likely that the patient will have

[9] Curlin and Tollefsen, *Way of Medicine*, 195.

done some homework on the internet, the library, or among friends to understand what osteoporosis is. But how much research is necessary? Which websites? How many journal articles? Which friends will know a lot about the diagnosis? For self-determination to be meaningful and in one's own best interests, it seems that some credible information is necessary.

The good news is that an experienced, licensed physician worthy of the profession will have had years of training and experience with patients who have had osteoporosis or will know to whom to refer the patient for the best care for osteoporosis. During the dance, the physician will help educate the patient about the diagnosis, the treatment modalities, and the prognosis associated with the condition. During that dance, the patient can ask questions, get clarifications, and situate her decision in the context of her own hopes, values, and goals. Together, the physician and patient can discover the best course of treatment for her, remembering that because she is the one with the condition, her decision is going to be influenced by her awareness or lack of awareness of the pain, suffering, or disability she is feeling as a result of the disease.

Respect for Conscience

What if the patient and the physician reach an impasse about the best treatment options? For instance, what if the adult Jehovah's Witness tells his doctor that his deeply held religious beliefs will not allow him to receive a blood transfusion? Both medicine and the law recognize the right of a patient to make decisions consistent with his or her conscience. In this case, at the least, the Jehovah's Witness patient would not receive a blood transfusion; but there is a range of options, and a healthy alternative would be found that is consistent with the patient's conscientious refusal of blood and blood products.

Patients are persons. As persons they have conscience rights. Physicians are persons too. Under the consumerist PSM discussed in this book, physicians may be viewed as obligated to provide the services the customer desires. Curlin and Tollefsen maintain that "in the PSM, informed consent gives way to informed choice: patients choose and physicians provide."[10] But this cannot be the way forward and at the same time preserve a covenantal profession of healing. Physicians must be allowed, as patients are, conscientiously to object to providing procedures and drugs they find violate their own deeply held religious beliefs, whether it is a refusal to perform elective abortions, offer puberty blockers to preadolescents, or provide lethal drugs for assisted suicides. Part of the position statement on Health Care Right of Conscience by the Christian Medical and Dental Associations observes:

> Christian healthcare professionals will sometimes need to disagree with patients, colleagues, or institutions over the ethical legitimacy of controversial medical practices. Under such circumstances, Christian healthcare professionals must be prepared to refuse to cooperate with such practices. They should do so with compassion and confidence, knowing that loving our neighbors sometimes means refusing to cooperate with their mistaken wishes. Conscience should be considered a right with profound ethical and religious importance. Therefore, Christian healthcare professionals should encourage colleagues, institutions, and

[10] Curlin and Tollefsen, 181.

governments to respect this right and to establish policies that accommodate clinicians who exercise it.[11]

In some ways the future of medicine is a return to the tradition that birthed the profession. Of course, the world has changed (a lot) since Hippocrates and those early Christians who adapted the Hippocratic Oath to make it more tenable to their beliefs and practice. But I have tried to offer convincing reasons why Christian-Hippocratism, or something like it, provides the ground and pillars for a medical ethics that celebrates and protects the sanctity of human life at both ends of life and in between. The way ahead in moral medicine sees the patient as an imager of God, medicine as a covenantal profession, and the aims of medicine a patient's health and flourishing, not an excarnational escape from our embodiment into a post-human future. Much more could be said, and much more has been said. At the end of this book, there is list of resources that provide next steps for those who want to know more.

Finally, I have had my fair share of experiences as a patient. I have danced the dance with physicians. In fact, as I was writing this book, I had major orthopedic surgery. Let us call it another layer of research for the book. As before, I came away from that experience not only with a new hip but also with a fresh appreciation for good doctors and good doctoring. I am grateful for those men and women who have followed their vocational calling to endure the educational rigors of medical training and to engage faithfully in the diligent practice of the healing arts. To paraphrase the Oath:

---

[11] "Conscience in Healthcare," p. 1, available for download at "Healthcare Right of Conscience," under "Individual Position Statement Abstracts with Full Statement Downloads" at CMDA, "Position & Public Policy Statements," CMDA.org, accessed October 14, 2024, https://cmda.org/policy-issues-home/position-statements/.

May you thrive and prosper in your fortune and profession, and may you be highly esteemed in the memory of your posterity.

Almighty God, whose Blessed Son Jesus Christ went about doing good, and healing all manner of sickness and disease among the people: Continue in our hospitals his gracious work among us; console and heal the sick; grant to the physicians, nurses, and assisting staff wisdom and skill, diligence and patience; prosper their work O Lord, and send down your blessing upon all who serve the suffering; through Jesus Christ our Lord. Amen.

Book of Common Prayer (2019)

RESOURCES

Bishop, Jeffery. *The Anticipatory Corpse: Medicine, Power, and the Care of the Dying*. Notre Dame, IN: University of Notre Dame Press, 2011.

Davis, Bill. *Departing in Peace: Biblical Decision-Making at the End of Life*. Phillipsburg, NJ: P&R, 2017.

Ferngren, Gary. *Medicine & Health Care in Early Christianity*. Baltimore: Johns Hopkins University Press, 2016.

———, and Ekaterina Lomperis. *Essential Readings in Medicine and Religion*. Baltimore: Johns Hopkins University Press, 2017.

Gawande, Atul. *Being Mortal: Medicine and What Matters in the End*. New York: Metropolitan Books, 2014.

Kalanithi, Paul. *When Breath Becomes Air*. New York: Random House, 2016.

Klass, Perri. *A Not Entirely Benign Procedure: Four Years as a Medical Student*. New York: Penguin, 1994.

Kaldjian, Lauris Christopher. *Practicing Medicine and Ethics: Integrating Wisdom, Conscience, and the Goals of Care*. New York: Cambridge University Press, 2014.

Lysaught, M. Therese, et al., eds. *On Moral Medicine: Theological Perspectives on Medical Ethics*. Grand Rapids: Eerdmans, 2012.

McKenny, Gerald P. *To Relieve the Human Condition: Bioethics, Technology, and the Body.* Albany: State University Press of New York, 1997.

Meilaender, Gilbert. *Bioethics: A Primer for Christians.* 4th ed. Grand Rapids: Eerdmans, 2020.

Orr, Robert D. *Medical Ethics and the Faith Factor: A Handbook for Clergy and Health-Care Professionals.* Grand Rapids: Eerdmans, 2009.

Shem, Samuel. *The House of God.* New York: Berkley, 2010.

Sloane, Andrew. *Vulnerability and Care: Christian Reflections on the Philosophy of Medicine.* London: T&T Clark, 2018.

Snead, Carter. *What It Means to Be Human: The Case for the Body in Public Bioethics.* Cambridge, MA: Harvard University Press, 2022.

Sulmasy Daniel P. *The Healer's Calling: A Spirituality for Physicians and Other Health Care Professionals.* New York: Paulist, 1997.

VanDrunen, David. *Bioethics and the Christian Life: A Guide to Making Difficult Decisions.* Wheaton, IL: Crossway, 2009.

SUBJECT INDEX

D

E

F

G

H

I

J

K

L

M

N

O

P

R

S

T

U

V

W

Z

SCRIPTURE INDEX